Advance Praise for *What Queen Esther Knew*

"When I'm faced with tasks demanding wisdom and courage far beyond my own, Esther's story reminds me to focus on what's most important in life."

—**Senator Elizabeth Dole**

"Connie Glaser and Barbara Smalley have done an excellent job of taking a story that was already timeless and making it even more relevant for women today."

—**Senator Debbie Stabenow**

"A fabulous tale of politics, leadership and ethics, Queen Esther's story is riveting. These leadership strategies resound as powerfully today as they did 2,000 years ago. A real triumph and gift for women everywhere."

—**Mark Victor Hansen,** Co-creator, #1 *New York Times* best-selling series *Chicken Soup for the Soul®*, Co-author, *The One Minute Millionaire*

"*What Queen Esther Knew* reaches back to Biblical times to draw important life lessons for any woman hoping to think bold and to do big. And there's plenty of learned wisdom from many of today's smartest female strategists. The book feels like the ultimate campfire confab of smart women; you'll leave energized!"

—**Nancy Evans,** Co-founder and Editor-in-Chief, iVillage

"Connie Glaser and Barbara Smalley teach us timeless and valuable strategies for surviving and prospering in the business world. This accessible volume should delight readers searching for personal fulfillment and growth."

—**Mary Sue Coleman,** President, University of Michigan

"Connie Glaser and Barbara Smalley make the story of Queen Esther relevant to the challenges women face in the workplace today. I know you'll learn valuable lessons that can help anyone develop their personal potential for leadership."

—**James E. Copeland, Jr.,** CEO, Deloitte & Touche, LLP

"Timeless advice from a timeless leader. Queen Esther knew then what years of analyzing effective executives have shown us now: To boost the odds of having a great leader, promote a female."

—**Joan E. Gerberding,** President, American Women in Radio and Television

"From making a Royal First Impression to the Royal Advice, Connie and Barbara have provided women with a roadmap to succeed and excel in leadership—both personally and professionally."

—**Bruce Nelson,** Chairman and CEO, Office Depot, Inc.

"We live in a time where the world is in desperate need of examples of courage, faith, and selflessness. We *need* to know what Queen Esther knew—now we do. Our challenge is to live up to the example."

—**Marilyn Carlson Nelson,** Chair and CEO, Carlson Companies

"I plan to give hundreds of *Queen Esther* books to my friends and colleagues, as I know the lessons learned will be discussed and cherished."

—**Edie Fraser,** President, Business Women's Network (BWN)

"The book wraps up the elements of leadership in a concise package and ties them with a big pink bow."

—**Toni Riccardi,** Chief Diversity Officer, Pricewaterhouse-Coopers

WHAT QUEEN ESTHER KNEW

BUSINESS STRATEGIES FROM A BIBLICAL SAGE

CONNIE GLASER
& BARBARA SMALLEY

AUTHORS OF <u>SWIM WITH THE DOLPHINS</u>

RODALE

Printed in the United States of America
Rodale Inc. makes every effort to use acid-free , recycled paper .

Book design by Joanna Williams

Library of Congress Cataloging-in-Publication Data

Glaser, Connie Brown.
    What Queen Esther knew : business strategies from a biblical sage / Connie Glaser and Barbara Smalley.
        p.   cm.
    Includes bibliographical references and index.
    ISBN 1–57954–690–0   hardcover
    1. Businesswomen—Religious life.   2. Esther, Queen of Persia.
3. Business—Religious aspects—Christianity.   I. Smalley, Barbara Steinberg.
II. Title.
BV4596.B8G57   2003
650.1'082—dc21   2003002293

Distributed to the book trade by St. Martin's Press
2 4 6 8 10 9 7 5 3 1   hardcover

Visit us on the Web at www.rodalestore.com, or call us toll-free at (800) 848-4735.

WE **INSPIRE** AND **ENABLE** PEOPLE TO IMPROVE
THEIR LIVES AND THE WORLD AROUND THEM

ACKNOWLEDGMENTS

Writing a book is a collaborative effort. In this, our fourth book together, we have grown to respect each other's strengths and talents even more. What began as a friendship over twelve years ago has evolved into a creative partnership, based on mutual admiration and trust.

Yet this book would never have found its voice were it not for our agent, Heide Lange. Thank you, Heide, for your professional know-how, unerring instincts, and uncompromising ethics. Your friendship is greatly valued.

Sincere thanks to our editor, Stephanie Tade, who realized the book's potential from the beginning and championed it on our behalf. The Rodale team is awesome; we are fortunate to have such an outstanding group of professionals in our corner and owe a debt of thanks to Marc Jaffe, Amy Rhodes, Cindy Ratzlaff, Cathy Gruhn, Mary Lengle, Lisa Dolin, Leslie Schneider, Dana Bacher, Kelly Schmidt, and Jackie Dornblaser.

We are especially grateful to our families who have helped us maintain a sense of balance and humor in our lives throughout this project. Our love and heartfelt thanks to our husbands, Tom and Tim. And to our sons, Russell and Max, Logan and Ben, thank you for the joy you've brought to our lives.

Growing up, we were fortunate to have exemplary parents—our own personal Mordecais—who mentored and encouraged us and instilled in us a strong sense of values and ethics. We are grateful to Dolly and Bernie Brown, and Zelda and

M. K. Steinberg for serving as role models and always providing love and support.

And how can a book be written without the support of close friends—who listened, encouraged, and provided laughter, the much-needed antidote to our stress. Many thanks to Richard Brown, Sandi Beals, Carol and Bob Deutsch, Cathy Carrabis, Krys and Ron Doerfler, Edie Fraser, Abe and Eileen Glaser, Carrie and Ron Ludwig, Bob Katz, Paul Karapetian, Sharon and Freddy Loef, Cindy Mann, Kathi McCarroll, Denny Marcus and Andre Schnabl, Ann Norwood, Vicki Nikiforov, Barbara Pomerance, Morene Seldes-Marcus, Marcia Stamell, and Joanne Swerdlin.

Thanks also to Joan and Sam Arazie, Amanda Barbour, Sandy Baumwald, Pat and Stu Chandler, Irene Daria, Katherine Duncan, Freida and Marvin Estroff, Willy and Jane Fowler, Holly and Laurie Fowler, Avra and Stan Hawkins, Judy and Dan Hees, Faye Hurwich, Marty Johnston, Kendra King, Murray Marcus, Lynn Massey, Kathy Rackley, Sue Rains, Karen and Neal Robinson, David Smalley, Ralph and Dot Smalley, Helen Sokoloff, Lois and Eugene Somberg, Gail and Kim Stearman, Dale Steinberg, Jack and Carol Steinberg, Mickey and Marilyn Steinberg, Debra Swinford, Clark Thomason, Elizabeth Tuggle, Warren Umansky, Patricia Villegas, Anna Walker, and Connie Wegmann for your love, support and for providing much-needed distractions. And to Ashlee Campbell and Jacob Rappoport, please know that your inspiration lives on.

We are grateful to the colleagues who have taken an interest and supported our "mission" through the years. With sincere appreciation and thanks to Nancy Alpert, Kate Bandos, Chris Brodnax, Lynn Connelly, Allison Cripps, Cathy Cox, Nancy Evans, Edna Farley, Joy Lynn Fields, Opal Haley, Pat Heim, Suzn

Head, Tammy Hughes, Kendall Kvicala, Monica Luechtefeld, Linda Muir, Toni Riccardi, Mary Ellen Rodgers, Shannon Scott, Erica Stephens, Dr. Jacqueline Taylor, Melissa Wahl, Marilyn Willison, Linda Wind, Marybeth Wydock, and Joanne Zukowski.

We are also most appreciative of modern-day Esthers who graciously shared their stories and advice with us: Sue Bixler, Evelyn Hannon, Avra Hawkins, Kathryn Hays, Marsha Londe, Carol Lopucki, Virginia Means, Astrid Pregel, Susan RoAne, Gwen Simmons, Betty Spence, Susan Varlamoff, and Sheila Wellington.

And to other chroniclers of Esther who inspired and provided us with insight in our research of this rich biblical story. We gratefully acknowledge the contributions of Michael V. Fox, Halls-Bascom Professor of Hebrew Studies at the University of Wisconsin at Madison; Carol Bechtel, Professor of Old Testament at Western Theological Seminary; Charles Swindoll, Chancellor of Dallas Theological Seminary; and Dianna Booher, author and CEO of Booher Consultants.

To Anne Ambrose and Dr. Arthur Cohen who provided moral and spiritual support throughout the course of this project.

And, finally, to Wattie Watkins, may she rest in peace, who made Connie her first Queen Esther costume.

CONTENTS

INTRODUCTION 3

THE STORY OF ESTHER 9

1

ASCENDING TO POWER:
MAKING A ROYAL FIRST IMPRESSION 13

2

FIND A MENTOR TO OPEN YOUR EYES
AND DOORS 37

3

IT PAYS TO KNOW THE PALACE GOSSIP 69

4

FIGHTING FOR WHAT YOU BELIEVE IN 83

5

MAPPING OUT YOUR PLAN OF ATTACK 107

6

COMMUNICATING WITH THE CLOUT
OF A QUEEN 129

7
DEALING WITH LIFE'S HAMANS 147

8
KEEPING THE FAITH 171

9
LET THE STORY BE TOLD 201

10
CELEBRATING YOUR OWN PERSONAL PURIM 219

AFTERWORD 229

REFERENCES 231

INDEX 255

WHAT
QUEEN ESTHER
KNEW

INTRODUCTION

You're going to fall in love with Esther. Then you're going to wonder
how you could have lived so long without realizing what a magnificent,
realistic and balanced message she models.

—*Charles R. Swindoll, author of* Esther: A Woman of Strength and Dignity

Chances are, you're familiar with the story of Queen Esther. If not, you are in for a treat. Hers is a remarkable tale told in the biblical book that bears her name. It's a brilliant, multifaceted story of palace intrigue and genocide narrowly averted by heroic rescue. It's an ancient but riveting rag-to-riches, tragedy-to-triumph tale that is as compelling as any work of fiction you'll find on today's best-seller list. Indeed, this gripping page-turner boasts all the ingredients to keep a reader hooked: a compelling and suspenseful plot, intriguing characters, a beautiful and courageous heroine, a nasty and despicable villain, romance, twists and turns—and, of course, a happy ending.

But as you know, Queen Esther's story is not fiction, Rather, it's a slice of history packed with principles that are still valid today. It's a Cinderella story that is truly timeless.

WHY QUEEN ESTHER?

The Bible is brimming with courageous and visionary women. So, why did we choose to focus on Queen Esther? For starters, in an age of political cynicism and dubious ethics, people today are clearly seeking heroes. Someone to admire . . . to look up to . . . to emulate as a role model. Women, in particular, have few heroes to emulate. Who better than Queen Esther?

She was a beautiful, powerful queen—smart, savvy, compassionate—who used her position of influence to save her people and change the course of history.

Even more compelling, Queen Esther managed to transform herself from an orphan girl in exile to the most powerful woman in the Persian Empire.

How did she rise to such heights of power in the ancient world? It's true, she was beautiful and used her comely ways to her advantage. But even more significantly, she was intelligent. She was a strategist. She was a persuasive speaker and a risk-taker who spoke up for what she believed in and asked for what she wanted. She studied palace politics to penetrate the inner circle of power. And she listened to her mentors to better understand how to influence others and use her authority to her advantage.

In short, Queen Esther emerges as an ideal role model for women today. Granted, her tale is ancient, but read on, and we think you'll be amazed to discover the many lessons and principles in her story that have great application for women in today's changing world.

Another reason we chose to use this magical story is its universal appeal. Indeed, the story of Esther is well known and loved by Jews and Christians alike. The Jewish holiday of Purim commemorates Esther's courageous triumph over Haman, with little girls dressing up as their heroine and proudly parading through the streets.

The story of Queen Esther is exalted by Christians as well. In fact, many Christian experts even suggest that the story of Esther and her willingness to sacrifice herself for her people parallels the story of Jesus.

Granted, non-Jews don't celebrate the holiday of Purim. But in her book on Queen Esther, titled *Interpretation: A Bible Commentary for Teaching and Preaching*, author Carol M. Bechtel believes that people of all faiths "would do well to remember the main event of that celebration—namely, the reading of the Book of Esther. This is a book, after all, about the struggle to be faithful in the midst of an increasingly unfaithful culture," she writes. "It is a story of courage, faith, and deliverance. In sum, it is a powerful work for the present . . . made even more powerful for its being written down."

What Did Queen Esther Know?

You probably know her story—or at least the gist of it. A Jewish orphan raised by her cousin Mordecai, Esther became queen of Persia and ultimately saved her people from annihilation. Few are aware, however, of the surprising parallels between the challenges and obstacles Esther faced and those facing women today. Neither are many privy to the modern-day lessons that can be gleaned from Esther's story.

When you first meet Esther, she appears one-dimensional. She is beautiful and kind, but superficial—not someone who belongs on a pedestal. And she appears passive—at least initially. When it comes to making important decisions, she defers to others. But this is not surprising, considering Esther's age and situation. "Her focus on superficials is to be expected of a young woman whose daily routine places overwhelming importance on her appearance," notes Michael V. Fox, author of *Character and*

Ideology in the Book of Esther. And, after all, she has lost her freedom, her home, her family.

As her story unfolds, however, Esther's transformation from an orphan girl to a true queen and leader is breathtaking. Slowly, she blossoms from someone who looks to others for all the answers to someone who designs and executes her own ideas and plans. And throughout this evolution, we see her become more comfortable with power—a challenge for most women.

Fox points out that Esther develops in three stages: "from passivity, to activity, to authority." Indeed, for the first half of her story, the men in Esther's life—the king, Mordecai, and Haman—appear to be the decision-makers. Yet, once she learns that the fate of her people lies in her hands, Esther's metamorphosis begins to reveal itself. *She* sends. *She* commands. *She* inquires.

Esther truly comes into her own when she realizes that she must stand up for what she believes in. Considering the corruption of ethics in business today, many modern-day Esthers struggle with these same issues involving integrity and remaining true to one's principles. So, there are valuable lessons to be learned from Esther's story. Taking calculated risks. Becoming a savvy strategist. Standing up for what you believe in. Communicating with clout. Summoning courage under fire.

And yet, not all the lessons we learn from Esther are somber ones. She knew the importance of royal appearance, working the palace grapevine, staying connected to her supporters, using feminine strengths to her advantage, listening as well as speaking clearly and directly, and celebrating one's success.

What *did* Queen Esther know? Plenty. And this book is filled with lessons— both big and small—that have relevance and value for women today.

In short, Queen Esther's legacy to the 21st century is enormous. As Dianna Booher, author of *The Esther Effect: The Seven Secrets of Confidence and Influence*, points out, "People of faith (both Jews and Christians) have been reading the Book of Esther for millennia and reacting in similar ways. Something about this book makes us all take stock of ourselves."

Elizabeth Dole agrees. In *Finding God at Harvard*, she acknowledges the powerful influence the story of Esther has had on her life. "While the particulars of her challenges may differ from those you and I face, the forces at work are as real as the moral is relevant," Dole writes. "The basic lessons Esther had to learn are lessons I needed to learn. Thus, the story of Esther, over the years, has taken on great significance for me. Indeed, it reflects an individual's discovery of the true meaning of life."

From orphan girl to one of the most powerful women in the world—how did Esther do it? And how can you emulate her success? In this book, we cover "the whole Megillah." As we've traveled around the country conducting seminars and interviews, we found women seeking practical solutions to everyday business concerns. We have included our best "Royal Advice" to these questions in each chapter. In addition, the book introduces you to 21st-century Queen Esthers and weaves together ancient wisdom and modern insights to provide inspiring, realistic, and above all, practical strategies to help you become the queen you deserve to be.

The Story of
Esther

*T*he story of Esther begins about 400 B.C.E. and is set in Persia. In the third year of his reign, King Ahasuerus decided to host a feast. On the seventh day of these festivities, the king summoned his queen, Vashti, to appear before him and demonstrate her beauty for all of his officials. When Vashti refused, the king was outraged. He subsequently banished her from the kingdom, and upon the advice of his advisors, launched a four-year search for her replacement.

The most beautiful maidens of the Persian Empire were brought to the palace for the king's consideration. One of these maidens was Esther, a Jewish orphan who had been raised by her older cousin, Mordecai, after her parents' death. Esther impressed all who met her, including King Ahasuerus, who chose her to be his queen.

Mordecai convinced Esther not to reveal her identity as one of the Jewish minority who had lived in Persia since the Exile. The two remained close even after she was crowned. In fact, each day, Mordecai would drop by the palace and ask after his cousin.

One day, while sitting near the palace gate, Mordecai overheard a plot to assassinate the king. He immediately told Esther, who reported it to the king in Mordecai's name.

Soon after that, the king promoted Haman, a descendant of Amelak, the traditional enemy of the Jews, to the position of chief advisor. Haman was a wicked and vain man who expected everyone to bow down to him. Mordecai, a pious Jew, refused to do so, which infuriated Haman. Not content to punish just Mordecai, Haman decided to destroy the entire Jewish population in Persia. He picked the dates for this holocaust by casting lots—or *purim*.

Through deception, Haman persuaded King Ahasuerus to go along with his plans to kill the Jews. And with the king's permission, Haman issued an edict proclaiming the 13th and 14th days of the Hebrew month of Adar as the designated time all Persian Jews would be slain. When Mordecai heard of this plan, he persuaded Esther to intercede on behalf of her people, although to approach her husband unbidden—and to identify herself as a Jew—could mean certain death.

Esther summoned her courage and entered the king's inner court dressed in her most royal garb. The king granted her an audience and promised her virtually anything she asked. Esther replied that she wished to invite the king and Haman to a banquet on that day. At the feast, she asked her guests to return for another banquet the following day.

Haman left the first banquet consumed with self-importance and pride. But these feelings quickly turned to rage when he saw Mordecai sitting at the palace gate and paying him no mind. Haman went home fretting about Mordecai's impudence. His wife, Zeresh, advised him to construct a gallows on which to hang Mordecai. Haman joyously acted upon this suggestion.

Haman's joy, however was short-lived. The following day— at Esther's second banquet—marked his downfall. There, Esther revealed Haman's villainous plot to kill all the Jews, along with the fact that she was Jewish herself. She then begged the king to "grant me my life and spare my people."

Outraged that someone would threaten his beloved queen, the king ordered that Haman be hanged on the very gallows intended for Mordecai. And although Persian law prevented the king from reversing his previous edict, he allowed Mordecai to issue a new edict permitting the Jews to defend themselves.

On the 13th and 14th days of Adar, the Jews were victorious against their enemies and saved from annihilation. Ever since, Jews have observed Purim at this time, a holiday filled with merrymaking, feasting, the re-telling of Esther's story, and saluting this heroine's incredible courage and faith. ♔

1

ASCENDING TO
POWER: MAKING
A ROYAL FIRST
IMPRESSION

*I*t all began with a domestic spat. In the third year of his
21-year reign, Ahasuerus, the powerful king of the Persian
Empire (which, at the time, included 127 provinces from
India to Ethiopia), was hosting a lavish week-long banquet.
Everyone present in Susa, the capital, was invited to attend. The
setting: the enclosed garden of the king's palace.

It was the social event of the season . . .

The garden had hangings of white and blue linen, fas-
tened with cords of white linen and purple material to
silver rings on marble pillars. There were couches of gold
and silver on a mosaic pavement of porphyry, marble,
mother-of-pearl and other costly stones. Wine was served
in goblets of gold, each one different from the other, and
the royal wine was abundant, in keeping with the king's
liberality. By the king's command, each guest was allowed
to drink in his own way, for the king instructed all the
wine stewards to serve each man what he wished.
—*Esther 1:6–8*

13

Meanwhile, Queen Vashti was hosting her own banquet for all the women in the palace.

On the seventh day of this feast, when the king was quite merry with wine, Ahasuerus commanded his eunuchs to bring Vashti before him so as to display her beauty for all to see. But Vashti, offended at the idea of being paraded as a mere possession alongside the king's other royal trappings, refused to come. This greatly enraged King Ahasuerus. And, as was customary, he asked the wise men of the court what he should do to punish his wife for disobeying him.

His advisors came up with a plan . . .

Let a search be made for beautiful young virgins for the king. Let the king appoint commissioners in every province of his realm to bring all these beautiful girls into the harem at the Citadel of Susa. Let them be placed under the care of Hegai, the king's eunuch, who is in charge of the women, and let beauty treatments be given to them. Then let the girl who pleases the king be queen instead of Vashti.
—*Esther 2:2–4*

In the search for a new queen, the beautiful Esther, an orphan girl who was being raised by her cousin Mordecai, was tapped to make the journey to the palace. Reluctantly, she complied, and at the court, she joined some 400 (historians estimate) other young maidens who spent the next year learning to look their best . . .

. . . six months with oil of myrrh and six with perfumes and cosmetics.
—*Esther 2:12*

All the maidens were entrusted to Hegai, the chief eunuch, whom Esther immediately befriended and became his favorite.

> Now the young lady pleased him and found favor with him. So he quickly provided her with her cosmetics and food, gave her seven choice maids from the king's palace, and transferred her and her maids to the best place in the harem.
> —Esther 2:9

After twelve months of beauty treatments, each maiden's turn to go before King Ahasuerus arrived. For each one participating in this ancient beauty pageant, the rules were the same. Whatever she requested—perfume, cosmetics, fine clothing, and jewelry—would be given to her to take from the harem to the king's quarters. But when Esther's turn came, she relied solely on Hegai's advice, requesting nothing other than what he suggested. She knew that Hegai, of all people, knew the king's social tastes. And so she deferred to the eunuch's advice.

Smart move. Ahasuerus was immediately smitten . . .

> Now the king was attracted to Esther more than to any of the other women, and she won his favor and approval more than any of the other virgins. So he set a royal crown on her head and made her queen instead of Vashti.
> —Esther 2:17–18

Esther's destiny hinged on making a royal first impression. Yours does too—and you don't have much time.

Four minutes. Studies tell us that's how long we have to make a first impression on somebody—be it a king, a potential new boss, an important new client, or a headhunter. In fact, within a mere ten seconds, that person will begin to make judgments about our sense of professionalism, social class, morals, and intelligence.

Researchers have also discovered that first impressions are often lasting ones. This means that when you play your cards right, you can enjoy the benefits of what sociologists call the "halo effect." In other words, if you're viewed positively within those critical four minutes, the person you've just met will likely assume that everything you do is positive.

Unfortunately, the reverse is also true. Boggle a first encounter with someone, and in most cases, that person will mistakenly assume that you have a slew of other negative traits and characteristics. Worse, the person is not likely to take the time or make the effort to reformulate a second or third impression of you.

"It's true," says Atlanta image consultant Susan Bixler, co-author of *5 Steps to Professional Presence*. "Those first few minutes of an encounter are basically indelible, and if you blow it, it's very difficult to erase that and start over."

The good news is, by deliberately cultivating a positive first impression, you can take advantage of the halo effect philosophy and avoid becoming the victim in a case of mistaken identity. Here's how.

LEARN "PALACE" PROTOCOL

Esther was crowned queen, in part, because she looked to Hegai to give her the inside scoop on the workings of the palace and the king's likes and dislikes. Her thinking: You can't win the game unless you know the rules.

Good strategy. Every kingdom—and every organization—has its own way of thinking and behaving. And if you want to succeed, it's critical that you understand these unwritten rules. Equally important is that you do all you can to adapt and fit in. Lone rangers rarely make a good first impression, nor do they typically succeed in the long run.

Today we call this critical process "understanding the corporate culture"—and it's timeless advice. Whether trying to get a foot in the door, land a promotion from within, call an important meeting, or negotiate a critical deal, it's imperative to understand that everyday routines and activities don't simply happen. Rather, they occur because of tradition, history, and expectations.

That, in a nutshell, defines corporate culture. It's the shared values of an organization—the politics or "glue" that holds a company together. It's what gives a firm focus and direction and what keeps every employee on the same page, pulling in the same direction. Understanding corporate culture not only gives you the inside track on management style and corporate identity, it reveals methods used in hiring, firing, and promoting staff and tells you how decisions are really made.

Trouble is, you're not likely to find all this neatly summarized in a company's annual report or outlined in its policies and procedures manual. Usually, you have to dig a little deeper. Company Web sites, for example, are often rich and revealing sources. Check there for clues about a firm's rituals, history, heroes, symbols, and jargon. While online, two other sites worth visiting include Wet Feet Press (www.wetfeet.com) and Vault Reports (www.vaultreport.com). Both are services that sell company dossiers geared to job applicants.

Paying close attention to a company's day-to-day operations should offer additional insight into its corporate culture. How are employees dressed? What about their work spaces? Do people have photos of their kids and plants on their desks, or are their work spaces strictly business-oriented? And what about their behavior? Are folks standing around the watercooler chatting, or are they sitting alone in their offices?

Doing a little detective work can help, too. Pinpoint who the superstars in the company are, then identify the personality traits and behaviors these people have in common.

Your best bet to mastering corporate culture, however, is to find your own Hegai. Form instant alliances with tenured colleagues who can give you a crash course on the subtleties of your new firm's environment—from values and beliefs to how people tend to interact with one another. Otherwise, you risk calling attention to yourself for all the wrong reasons.

"When I was first named vice chief of radiology, I started attending Medical Executive Committee meetings," says Dr. Kathleen McCarroll, first female chief of staff at Detroit Receiving Hospital. "Eager to participate, I would either come up with an idea, or there would be an agenda item, and I would put my hand up and start discussing it. But no one else would discuss it. In fact, no one else ever said anything. And whenever there was a motion on the floor, there would essentially be no discussion. Everyone would just put their hand up and vote. I couldn't figure it out."

Finally, McCarroll's boss gave her some advice. "Never surprise anyone at a meeting. Never bring up something that hasn't been discussed before the meeting. If you're going to make a motion or build on an agenda item, you must discuss it with all the other pertinent parties before the meeting."

"What I learned is that while it may be a sham democracy, this is the way a lot of boards work," McCarroll continues. "If you go to a meeting and make a motion during new business, ten-to-one, the motion gets tabled because nobody's had time to jawbone it around outside of the public forum. But even worse, by speaking up before conferring with others, you show everyone that you're out of the loop . . . out of the power structure."

ROYAL ADVICE

Job interviews make me nervous. I've learned how to pre-pare for them, however, and once I get comfortable, I usually do very well. Still, that inevitable first question—"Tell me about yourself"—always throws me for a loop. What's the best way to respond so that I make a positive first impression right away?

This common warmup question can be a difficult one to answer because it is so broad. But your response to it in terms of making a positive first impression is especially important because the "four-minute rule" is in effect.

The real question here is: "How does your past/current work experience/education/volunteer activites, etc. qualify you for this position?" So, the best way to answer this ice-breaker is to prepare—and rehearse—an executive sum-mary that highlights your key accomplishments, your strengths, and how these feats will be of value to your would-be employer.

This is not the time to ramble, so keep your introduction brief—60 to 90 seconds should suffice. But do make sure that your summary packs a powerful punch. For example: "I have ten years of experience in management, including seven years overseeing a sales staff of 150 people who con-sistently met—or exceeded—their quotas. I adjust well to new environments, and I'm a motivator. As this year's United Way chair, for example, I helped our company raise a record amount of money."

DRESS TO TAKE OVER THE THRONE

In recent years, the concept of business casual has swept the country. Yet, researchers and modern-day Queen Esthers alike agree that no matter what a company's dress code says, many of the old rules still apply.

Right or wrong, fair or not, when it comes to making a royal first impression—or catching the eye of your superiors—what you wear remains almost as important as how you perform. And dressing for the job you want—not the job you have—can still enhance your status.

Esther, for example, knew that she—like all the other young maidens in the harem—had but once chance to impress King Ahasuerus. So, wisely, she studied the palace culture, heeded Hegai's advice, and donned royal robes to look the part of a queen.

Twenty-plus years of research by John T. Molloy, author of the best-selling *New Woman's Dress for Success*, offers proof positive that the right clothing can give you a decisive competitive edge. In fact, in his studies, Molloy has found that dressing for success appears to be a factor in promotion even when you don't have a lot of contact with the public. "A prime example of this were women scientists who worked in seven different laboratories," he writes. "These women never saw or were seen by anyone but their co-workers and bosses, and some saw them only occasionally. They and their supervisors believed that all that counted was the quality of their work. Yet, even in those settings, those who dressed like professionals, not back-room researchers, were twice as likely as their equally talented sisters to move into supervisory positions."

A polished presence offers other benefits as well. It helps you to project authority and gain respect from colleagues and clients. It can even elevate your status among your subordinates.

Avra Hawkins' promotion from radiation therapist to department head at a major Atlanta hospital was totally unexpected. "It wasn't a position I applied for, nor aspired to," she says. "Yet, when three other staffers left at the same time, I was the obvious choice. Not only was I in-house, I also had the right degree for the job. Suddenly, however, I was in charge of a $500,000 annual budget and had all kinds of new administrative responsibilities for which I was ill prepared."

A quick study, Hawkins fared well in her new position, but since she had no intentions of climbing the ranks any farther, it never dawned on her to dress differently for her new role. "Since I would occasionally have to step in and treat patients, I continued to wear my hospital uniform, although I would always put on a lab coat when I had to attend administrative meetings," she recalls.

All that changed when Hawkins' administrative assistant attended an in-service training session at the hospital that covered, among other topics, professional image. "She came back from training and told me that part of what she'd learned was that when a person moves up, they need to look the part," Hawkins reports. "'No need to get too fancy,' she assured me, 'but they do encourage people at your level to wear suits.'"

Hawkins decided to try an experiment and exchanged her lab coat for a jacket at departmental meetings. She was amazed at the results that occurred by this change. "I realized that my people began to show me more respect. Many also mentioned that they were proud of the new image I was projecting on their behalf. At department head meetings, my credibility increased. Colleagues started paying more attention to me and the ideas I'd bring up. Moreover, on a personal level, I began to feel more confident and in-charge."

Bottom line: If you ignore a company's dress code, it's likely to cost you. And the price you'll pay? "You'll be seen as an outsider to the power structure," believes Anna Navarro, founder of Work Transitions, a nationwide organization based in St. Louis that trains career strategists and helps people find fulfillment in their work. And it may limit your opportunity for moving up.

Not that choosing to dress on your own terms is necessarily a bad thing. It may simply mean you don't fit the organization's culture or belong in your current job. As Navarro points out, "If you chafe under the prevailing dress code—whether it's too casual or too traditional—your resistance might be indicative of more telling issues about how you feel about your job."

For example, Navarro recently had a client who was a high-ranking executive at a major telecommunications firm. "Her managerial position required a wardrobe of grays, blacks, and dark blues, but her personal style yearned for bright yellow, purples, and oranges. When we analyzed her skills and ideal working conditions, it turned out her strongest suit was creativity." Recognizing that her job was an ill fit, this woman ultimately decided to pursue a different career path. "Now she works as a freelance creator of training workshops," Navarro adds. "Her office looks like an art studio, and she does her best work in this setting."

CARRY YOURSELF LIKE A QUEEN

In a landmark study of communications, UCLA sociolinguist Albert Mehrabian, Ph.D., discovered that when you first meet someone, the impact you make depends just seven percent on the words you use and thirty-eight percent on your tone of voice and inflection. What about the remaining fifty-five percent? It comes from nonverbal communication—your body language. And that includes facial expressions, gestures, and posture.

"Your body language won't land you a job, but it could tip the impression scale in your favor," says Bixler. "Even if you're going for a promotion, you need to have a presence that shows you deserve it—and that means you must look, behave, and have the nonverbal communication skills of someone at that next level or that higher salary."

The good news is, when you're trying to make a positive first impression on someone, there are several ways to use Mehrabian's formula to your advantage.

For starters, keep in mind that posture is paramount. Maybe in Esther's day, a submissive stance was appropriate for women, particularly when addressing a king. But in the 21st century, slouching, lowering your head, and casting your eyes downward are nonverbal blunders that can sabotage your credibility.

Instead, assume a royal pose by standing like a queen and holding your head high—to keep your crown intact. Also, watch the head bobbing. In addition to loosening your crown, it can make you look girlish, or infer that you agree with what someone is saying—even when you may not!

Royals also know they're entitled to space. And if you want to appear regal, you need to take up more of it. It's a fact that leaders take up more space than others do. In one study, when volunteers were asked to rate videotaped subjects, 80 percent considered those who used more space around them—by leaning slightly forward, keeping their palms and arms open, putting their elbows on a chair or table, or appearing relaxed—as intelligent, confident, and powerful.

Women more than men, however, tend to shrink into their spaces. Fortunately, this is an easy fix. Instead of clenching your fist, open it. Instead of holding your hands in a tight grasp, tent the fingertips. Instead of sitting with your hands tightly folded, drape them loosely over the arm of the chair. So, rest easy on your throne, and take up the space you're entitled to.

MAKE A GRAND ENTRANCE

A queen knows how to enter a room: by smiling graciously, making eye contact, greeting people by name, and extending their hand. But equally important to making a grand entrance is entering a room with purpose. To pull this off, Debra A. Benton, author of *Lions Don't Need to Roar: Using the Leadership Power of Professional Presence to Stand Out, Fit In, and Move Ahead,* recommends taking a quick power pause before entering a room. "A split-second pause gives you more status and possibly more respect," she believes. "By doing this, you nonverbally announce, 'I'm here. I'm ready. I know who I am, and I know what I'm doing.'"

But don't dally too long in the doorway. Proceed directly to a seat or approach others with enthusiasm. Tentative behavior, such as poking your head in a room first or seeming unsure what to do when you enter, can work against you.

Once you've made your entrance, make your every move count. Generally speaking, the fewer movements you make, the more powerful, deliberate, credible, and intelligent you're perceived to be. In a videotaped study of how women and men entered a room to a meeting, the women exhibited an average of twenty-seven different major movements; the men, only twelve.

A woman, for example, might take off her coat, set down her files, adjust her hair and clothes, pull business cards, a pen, or other items from her purse—and so on. Sounds innocent enough, but observers of the tape believed that women took longer to be composed, and this distracted attention from what they said in the meeting!

Something else to watch out for: "yelling" with your hands. In conversations, women tend to "hand dance" when making a point. In fact, studies show that women use twice the number of hand gestures that men do. You may feel as if you're just being expressive, but excessive hand gestures can distract from the impact you're trying to make and cause you to look nervous. Worse, when your hand gestures don't match and confirm the point you're verbalizing, not only will they diminish the strength of your delivery, they can be confusing and contradictory.

Consider the case of a 41-year-old Midwestern woman in the running for a senior-level management position at a Fortune 1000 high-tech firm. "On paper, she was our top candidate," reports the recruiter who managed the search assignment. "Her résumé was first class: an MBA from an Ivy League university, superior technical skills, and international management experience. On the phone, she sounded equally impressive—polished, poised, and dynamic."

But when the woman showed up for a face-to-face interview, the recruiter knew she wasn't a good fit. "She was overly animated and used large and confusing gestures," he says. "And when I talked, she would nod her head—nonstop. Verbally, she did a pretty good job of selling herself, but between those extreme gestures and that constant head bobbing, it was tough to take her seriously."

ESTABLISH A ROYAL PRESENCE

When industrial psychologists recently analyzed the performance evaluations of some 61,000 senior-level executives, they were astonished by the results: Female managers ranked higher than their male counterparts in almost every measure except confidence—and confidence is key to royal presence. The good news is, confidence is easier to develop than competence.

These findings were no fluke! In fact, the researchers were studying the qualities of strong leaders; they weren't even looking at gender differences. What's more, the evaluations they analyzed came from a wide diversity of companies—high-tech, health care, financial services, manufacturing, and consumer goods. Plus, many of these executives had been evaluated by up to two dozen people, including their bosses, peers, and subordinates.

Women's strengths? Some came as no surprise. For example, female executives scored higher in areas such as "motivating others," "fostering communication," "goal-setting," and "listening to others."

But many stereotypes were shattered as well. Women also outperformed men at "producing high-quality work," "recognizing trends," and "generating new ideas and acting on them."

Obviously, women have the right stuff to run America's top companies. So, why aren't more of them at the helm? What's missing? Perhaps the very quality that set Esther apart from all the other women vying to be queen—a royal presence.

Okay, so maybe 21st-century recruiters call it "executive presence," but it's as important today as it was in Esther's time. And it matters just as much as—maybe even more than—impeccable credentials and an impressive track record. It may even compensate for résumé weaknesses.

In fact, headhunters estimate that, on average, executive presence accounts for as much as 70 percent of first impressions we make. But that figure applies to men. Throw a highly qualified female into the mix, and that figure soars to 85 percent. As former Texas governor Ann Richards once quipped, "Ginger had to do everything that Fred did—only backwards and in high heels."

What's more, in recent years, executive presence has emerged as such an essential prerequisite for career advancement that major corporations like Shell Group and J. P. Morgan Chase have sent many of their high-potential female managers to special seminars to develop this elusive quality, reports *Business Week* columnist Michelle Conlin.

What exactly *is* executive presence? "Think of it as a frame around all your credentials and experience," says Bixler. "If you don't have good professional presence, it's almost like having a terrific painting with a lousy frame. And what the lousy frame will do is detract from the beauty of the painting. But what a great frame will do is add to it."

Executive presence is appearance, posture, and poise, for sure. It's also body language, facial expression, and communication skills. Typically, people with executive presence enter a room expecting to "take focus," says Sharon Voros, president of Voros Communications in Fort Worth, Texas. "They move crisply, but gracefully. They make the first move to shake hands and lean forward slightly when they sit. They're able to lead 30 to 45 seconds of small talk (about the weather, sports, travel) with ease, and they use the other person's name periodically when making points—but not so much that they sound like a salesperson."

Adds Conlin, "Executive presence refers to that ability to take hold of a room by making a polished entrance, immediately shaking people's hands, and forging quick, personal connections instead of defaulting to robotic formalism and shrinking into a chair. When leaders with executive presence speak, people listen—because the talk is filled with conviction instead of equivocation."

But executive presence encompasses a lot of "intangibles" as well. Jay Gaines, CEO of Jay Gaines & Co., a well-respected New York executive firm, defines it as "a combination of self-confidence, passion, energy, and enthusiasm. But it's got to be genuine." In a nutshell, executive presence is a special sparkle, a personal magnetism. It's charisma coupled with knowledge, know-how, character, skill, experience, and nobility of purpose.

Naturally, we're attracted to people with executive presence. "That's because they're positive, and because they have vision, and because they have energy, expertise, and confidence in what they're saying and doing is right," believes Tony Alessandra, Ph.D., author of *Charisma: Seven Keys to Developing the Magnetism That Leads to Success*. And naturally, people who possess this quality are almost always super-successful. That's because, by its very nature, executive presence gives you power and influence over others, Alessandra adds.

The good news is, executive presence isn't something you're born with; rather, you develop and cultivate it by:

Walking the walk. Bill Gaul, president of the Destiny Group, a search firm in San Diego that specializes in recruiting ex-military officers for business positions, sees many female candidates leave the service for high-level jobs in Corporate America. "Executive presence is rarely an issue with former military officers," he says. "These women know how to carry themselves so they look confident and self-assured. They glide, as if they have a purpose in life."

Walking the talk. Cynthia Scott, a partner with San Francisco–based executive consulting firm Changeworks, says she's astounded at how often female managers with the potential to advance will leave a meeting without having said much—if anything. "That makes them come off as passive and unengaged," she says. Worse, when they do speak up, many women blow it by using qualifiers or ending their sentences with the inflection of a question—"a move that causes people to doubt what they're saying," she adds.

Planning ahead. It's hard not to admire people with executive presence. They seem to have that natural ability to think fast on their feet. Yet, as Ruth Gordon once said, "The best impromptu speeches are the ones written well in advance." Susan Wilson Solovic, author of *The Girls' Guide to Power and Success*, agrees. People with executive presence never "wing it," she says. "They think about what they are going to say before an important interview, major meeting, big presentation, or critical networking event. They do their homework and know in advance what will be covered and who will be in attendance. They take notes and rehearse the points they want to make. They also anticipate comments and questions from others, considering in advance how they'll respond. That way, they won't be searching for appropriate ways to articulate their ideas. And their conversation won't be cluttered with 'uhms' and 'uhs,' ensuring that their message makes more of an impact."

When trying to land a position as director of human resources for a multibillion-dollar firm, Virginia Means knew she faced an uphill battle because of her young age—32. "Once I had made it through the interviews with the executive search firm, I was scheduled to meet with the CEO and his top team," she recalls. "I was incredibly nervous and knew that to be successful, I had to project the confidence of someone a decade my senior. So, I sought counsel from a male mentor, who served as my 'image consultant.' He gave me great advice far beyond the 'polish your shoes' and 'wear a suit that's in sync with the company's culture.'"

That advice included doing her homework on each executive in the company—"finding out as much as I could about their hot buttons, then mapping my skills and experience to their concerns," she says. "The Internet is a great place to begin that kind of research, and if you believe in six degrees of separation, you are

ROYAL ADVICE

I just had a very promising job interview and feel certain that I will be invited back for a second round. I know there were several other candidates scheduled for interviews after mine. What can I do to follow up and reinforce the positive first impression I made?

Send a thank-you note to your interviewer(s) right away. Few candidates (just ten percent) take the time to do this, so it's a great way to separate yourself from the competition. In addition to expressing gratitude, you can use this follow-up correspondence (both hand-written notes and e-mails are acceptable) to restate your interest in the position, add anything pertinent you may have forgotten to mention in your interview, review your strengths, and reinforce why you are the best person for the job.

bound to have a connection with someone in the company who can act as an information source."

Her mentor also advised Means to drive a "nice executive car" to the interview. "The problem was I'd been driving the same car for almost a decade. It was in fine shape, but in no way could it be considered a 'royal coach!'" she laughs. Means ended up borrowing a friend's BMW to drive to the breakfast interview, and was grateful she did. "Afterwards, one of the executives asked if I could drop him off at the office. It was no surprise that he had the same type car (his was in the shop). I found out that he had a love for cars—especially BMWs—and that made for a wonderful chat. He got to talk about himself, and the focus was off me for a while."

The Credibility Quotient

King Ahasuerus was smitten the moment he met Esther. Obviously, she immediately impressed him as someone who was exactly what he was looking for in a queen. How did she do it? Granted, she was beautiful, but surely she possessed some other quality that made her stand out in the competition to be queen.

Esther had credibility. *Something* about her made the king realize that she was honest, trustworthy, and deserving of the crown he bestowed upon her.

Fast forward to the 21st century, and credibility remains a prerequisite for success. When we are credible, others have confidence in our leadership abilities. When we are credible, we earn the respect, trust, and support of everyone around us—our superiors, our colleagues, and our subordinates.

Trouble is, although women are moving faster than ever into corporate positions, credibility issues are still an obstacle. In one recent survey, for example, 10,000 men and women were asked, "What are the major disadvantages for females in your workplace?" Their consensus: Both male and female respondents agreed that women generally fall short on credibility.

Many do have it, of course. Think Barbara Walters. With her casual grace—and killer instinct—she has interviewed the biggest names in politics, business, and entertainment and gotten straight answers to the toughest and most personal questions. How does she do it? People open up to her because they respect and trust her. She has, in a word, credibility.

Katie Couric has it, too. This chipper but tough-as-nails

anchor on *The Today Show* has established her credibility in hard-hitting interviews with such public figures as former First Lady Barbara Bush, Colin Powell, Hillary Rodham Clinton, Secretary of Defense Donald Rumsfeld, and General Norman Schwarzkopf. Off-camera, she has made herself even more credible by working tirelessly to increase awareness of colon cancer.

The trouble with credibility is that it typically takes time to establish. But when trying to make a positive first impression—say, in a job interview—there isn't a lot of time. (Remember the four-minute rule?)

Not a problem. In fact, there are numerous strategies you can use to establish instant credibility:

Match your communication style to those of your interviewer. When it was Esther's turn to meet the king, she knew that to make a good impression, she needed to adopt a style very different from her predecessor, Vashti. She also knew that to be chosen as queen, she needed to find a way to communicate with the king in such a way that he would feel instantly comfortable with her.

A job hunter in today's business world needs to do the same—figure out the interviewer's style and adapt accordingly. Cynthia Phillips, a regulatory field director for AstraZeneca Pharmaceuticals in Wilmington, Delaware, says she developed this skill with the help of her career coach, Anne Warfield of Impression Management Professionals in Minneapolis.

"I had worked at Astra and was trying to get hired by the newly-merged company," Phillips explains. "Anne taught me clues for discerning communication styles. For example, one type of communicator—the 'connector'—likes to talk about personal matters and displays family photos in the office. An 'analyzer' on the other hand, is focused on content and prefers to skip the chitchat."

To practice sizing up an interviewer's style and adjusting her manner accordingly, Phillips did lots of role-playing. Soon after, she had eight interviews for other jobs, and each time, she applied what she had learned. Her strategy paid off. Phillips landed the job she wanted most and has since been promoted.

Balance your body language. "If your body language is apologetic—if you lack eye contact, don't extend your hand right away, are hesitant about where to sit, or are basically acting like you're taking up someone's time—that can set the tone that you don't have a whole lot to offer," says Bixler. "On the flip side, being overly aggressive—claiming too much space, having the volume of your voice too loud, not being able to sort of mirror and match what the environment is—will also certainly work against you. So there's a balance you have to strike."

Focus on showing that you can do the job. "Be prepared to highlight the steps that you would take to solve the employer's problem and to reach the employer's goal," advises Lebanon, New Jersey, headhunter Nick A. Corcodilos, online host and author of *Ask the Headhunter*. "Show the manager how you think and how you work. Be ready to tackle the issue of profitability: How is your way of doing this work going to reduce costs or increase revenues? Put a number on it. The number doesn't have to be exactly right, but you should be prepared to defend it intelligently."

Before she was tapped to take over as chairman and CEO of Avon, Andrea Jung was working for the cosmetics company as president of product marketing for the U.S. While in that position, she decided to become an Avon Lady herself. "To get a grip on our customers' desires, as well as the struggles of our sales force, I needed to go through the selling experience myself," she explains. "So, I went door-to-door in my neighborhood and did a lot of listening."

Smart move. By the time she took over as CEO, Jung knew all of Avon's failings firsthand—*and* how to fix them.

The bottom line is, credibility is definitely coachable. Perhaps nowhere is that more evident than at Springboard Enterprises. This national nonprofit venture is dedicated to helping women get their fair share of equity capital for new start-up ventures. Several times a year, Springboard recruits the best and brightest female entrepreneurs who are seeking venture capital and sends them to eight-week "boot camps." There, they are paired with coaches, investors, strategists, lawyers, and financial consultants devoted to helping them strengthen their presentations to venture capitalists—primarily men.

The women chosen ultimately present their start-up companies at a forum packed with scores of potential investors who have the power to give them the funding they need. Thus, five weeks of boot camp are spent rehearsing their pitch and polishing their image so they'll come across as credible.

Results? The Springboard Project has been an enormous success. To date, nearly 40 percent of Springboard's graduates have raised in excess of $700 million from VCs and angels.

Annette Gilchrist, Ph.D., is one Springboard success story. Formerly a professor of molecular pharmacology and biological chemistry at Northwestern University, Gilchrist—along with fellow scientist Heidi Hamm, Ph.D.—founded Cue BIOtech in June 2000. The company came about after this pair of professors developed a process to identify small molecules that work inside cells to block diseases. "These molecules can be developed into drugs to treat patients with heart disease, cancer, AIDS, and other illnesses," says Gilchrist.

Cue BIOtech applied for patents, leased office and laboratory space on Northwestern's medical school campus, and began searching for money to get the business running. With a sluggish economy permeating the venture capital market, however, Gilchrist knew that coming across as credible was critical for attracting investors. "That's where Springboard helped," she says. "I'm happy and most comfortable doing science. The business side is where I'm nervous."

Cue BIOtech was among 230 applicants submitting business plans to Springboard—and one of 26 chosen to make a ten-minute presentation to VCs.

But before that happened, Gilchrist was coached extensively on delivery, critiqued by a panel of venture capitalists, and given tips on what to wear. Their advice was invaluable, as it pinpointed weaknesses Gilchrist wasn't even aware of, thus enhancing her presence and credibility. "They told me to talk more about the company and less about the science, keep my hands out of my pockets, and wear a jacket because it's more business-like," she recalls.

When it was show time, Gilchrist didn't disappoint. To hide her nervousness, she opened with a joke: "You've all heard that the trick for a speaker is to imagine that her audience is naked. Well, I'm imagining that you're all wearing lab coats."

The VCs loved the joke, allowing Gilchrist to relax and get on with her PowerPoint presentation summarizing the company's goals and five-year financial forecast. "The Springboard experience generated incredible publicity," she reports. "A week later, I was invited to Kalamazoo, Michigan, to give a similar presentation to 100 Michigan venture capitalists. A few days after that, I repeated it for a Chicago VC." Cue BIOtech has since received a considerable monetary investment and show of confidence from the VC community. "Not a bad start," Gilchrist adds. And that is just the beginning. ♛

2

FIND A MENTOR
TO OPEN YOUR EYES
AND DOORS

*H*egai served as Esther's mentor in the palace, grooming her to meet King Ahasuerus and familiarizing her with the subtleties of court protocol. Esther soaked up the privileged information and benefited from Hegai's tutelage and insider status.

Yet an even more important influence in Esther's life was her cousin Mordecai. Following the death of Esther's mother and father, Mordecai took Esther under his wing and raised her as a daughter.

A man of principle and courage, Mordecai served as a powerful role model for Esther, influencing her development of values, morality, and faith. Mordecai was a man of great intelligence and a member of the prestigious Sanhedrin (the "Supreme Court" and legislative body of the Jewish people) one of the qualifications of which was the ability to speak 70 languages. Through Mordecai's guidance and encouragement, Esther reaped the benefits—unusual for a girl in biblical times—of her guardian's education.

Mordecai was also politically savvy and had lots of connections with palace personnel. This being "in the loop" ultimately enabled

*him to forewarn Esther of potential dangers as well as advise her
what to do.*

*Needless to say, Mordecai fretted when Esther was taken to the
palace to be considered for queen. In fact, he counseled her to keep
quiet about her religion and genealogy until the time was right . . .*

> **Esther had not revealed her nationality and family back-
> ground because Mordecai had forbidden her to do so.
> Every day he walked back and forth near the courtyard
> of the harem to find out how Esther was and what was
> happening to her.**
> **—*Esther 2:10–11***

*Esther was wise to heed her mentor's advice, and doing so ulti-
mately allowed her to save her people.*

*Even after she was chosen as queen, Esther remained loyal to
Mordecai and still listened to and accepted his advice. Theirs was a
relationship based on mutual trust and respect, and the two not only
shared a bond of kinship and friendship, but worked extremely well
together as a team.*

*Ultimately, Mordecai was responsible for Esther's reluctantly
stepping out of her comfort zone and confronting the most critical
decision of her life. With Mordecai's support and guidance, Esther
evolved from a humble orphan girl into a woman of integrity and
substance—and emerged as the most powerful woman in the world
at that time.*

Mentors are just as important today as they were in Esther's
time—perhaps even more so for women. In one recent study involving 159 female and 151 male executives in Fortune 1000
companies, nearly two-thirds of the women said they had been
mentored, compared to fewer than one-half of the men. What's
more, of the women surveyed who were CEOs or presidents of
their companies, a whopping 75 percent had been mentored.

Even women who had climbed the corporate ladder and landed their current position without the benefit of having a mentor mentioned that prior mentoring had given them the confidence in themselves and the skills they needed to attain the position on their own.

"In my experience, the single most important reason why—among the equally talented—men tend to rise higher than women is that most men have mentors and most women do not," says Sheila Wellington, author (with Betty Spence and the staff of Catalyst) of *Be Your Own Mentor*. Her opinion is confirmed by more than 30 years of research on women and their work conducted by Catalyst—the nation's preeminent source of information on women in the workplace—which Wellington heads. "Mentors are more important to career success than hard work, more important than talent, more important than intelligence. Why? Because you need to learn how to operate in the work world—whether in a corporation, a professional firm, a nonprofit, a university, or the public sector—and mentors can teach you how."

Indeed, the benefits of having a seasoned someone take you under his or her wing are legion. Mentors can provide sponsorship, guidance, and feedback, as well as create unique learning opportunities for you. They can serve as sounding boards, cheerleaders, role models, and confidants. Mentors are also there to confirm, counsel, challenge, and encourage you to reach your full potential.

Decades of studies offer solid proof that mentored individuals enjoy a host of perks: They perform better on the job, advance more rapidly within an organization, report higher job and career satisfaction, and express lower turnover intentions than their nonmentored counterparts.

Not surprisingly, researchers have also found that mentors can be especially beneficial to women. Like it or not, when it comes to breaking through the proverbial glass ceiling and achieving coveted jobs traditionally held by men, women still need an extra push—and having a mentor can make a huge difference.

For example, executive women recently polled by Deloitte & Touche said their mentors most helped them by:

- Offering words of encouragement (90 percent)
- Showing interest in their careers (80 percent)
- Looking for projects to highlight their protégés' abilities (75 percent)
- Counseling them on long-term goals (66 percent)
- Including them in meetings and networking events (60 percent)

The problem is, many women don't actively seek mentors. Instead, they wait to be chosen. Or, they fall into mentoring relationships without fully understanding the concept and are not comfortable being coached. Among the key findings of a nationwide study conducted by The Leader's Edge Research and involving 341 Fortune 500 and other executives with salaries of $100,000 and above: 79.4 percent of women utilized mentors as protective allies rather than using them for help in obtaining assignments and gaining visibility.

SOME THINGS NEVER CHANGE

Esther had Mordecai—the older cousin who served as a father to her when she lost her parents—as a mentor. Throughout history, many famous women have also credited their success, in large part, to their dads: Elizabeth Cady Stanton, Eleanor Roosevelt, Mary Shelley, and Anna Freud, to name a few. In fact, while researching their pioneering book *The Managerial Woman*, Margaret Henning and Anne Jardim—cofounders of the business school at Simmons College—found that the top 25 female achievers in American business shared something unusual in common: All had fathers who encouraged them to excel.

That trend continues, according to John Davis, a Harvard Business School senior lecturer. "Wherever I go, most of the women I meet between 30 and 50 tell the same story," he told the *New York Times*. "They say they had successful, supportive fathers who were the ones to tell them to go out there and get 'em."

Davis, whose specialty is family-owned business, also notes that fathers' attitudes are drastically changing. "That very old tradition of automatically handing down the family enterprise to the first born son is waning. There is a growing willingness to give it over to the most competent child, regardless of whether she is female."

Such was the case for Alexandra Lebenthal, who was tapped to take over as president and CEO of Lebenthal & Company, a municipal-bond-brokerage firm, in 1995. "I think the other two kids were bored by the business," James Lebenthal, her father, said in an interview with the *Princeton Alumni Weekly*. Plus Alexandra "was authoritative and commanding."

"I always joke that I was the only one who listened (to the banter about mutual funds) at the dinner table," quipped Alexandra in an interview with the *New York Times*. She says she never felt any pressure to follow in her father's footsteps. "It wasn't like we'd visit his office, and he'd say, 'One day, this will all be yours.' He told us to find whatever it was that we were passionate about."

From early childhood, Lebenthal was impressed with her father's profession. "I remember him taking us down to the World Trade Center to watch it being built," she says, "and talking to us about how they got the money to build it. My dad had a passion about saving and investing in America and how it made for a better and more productive country. That sunk in with me."

Lebenthal also remembers working with her father at an early age. "When I was in fifth grade, New York City was in a fiscal crisis, and my dad launched a campaign to prove that shoring up the municipal bond market was important for small investors," she recalls.

To make his point, James Lebenthal recruited his daughter and a couple of her friends to spend an entire Saturday at his office adding up the par value of all the general-obligation NYC bonds. "The goal was to determine how many individuals were holding these bonds, and the task—sifting through piles and piles of carbon copies of confirmation of trades—was grueling," she reports.

But well worth the effort. "With our help, my dad came up with the number of 160,000 owners of bonds who would be adversely affected by default or bankruptcy. The idea was, these weren't fat cats and rich people who would be affected."

In return for their services, James Lebenthal "paid" the girls in skeins of colorful telephone wire, which, at the time, was all the rage for making jewelry. "What I remember is two things," Alexandra says. "First, that he trusted me to do the job. Second, that he was tuned in enough to me to know, without me telling him, exactly what we prized. That's always stayed with me."

Later, as a college student at Princeton, Alexandra dreamed of becoming an actress, but working summers at the family firm changed her mind. "I was intrigued by business as viewed from a historical, sociological, and anthropological perspective."

After graduating, she chose to work outside the family company—at Kidder Peabody—first. "The plan was to get both more life experience and more business experience," she explains. Now, at the helm of Lebenthal & Company, she insists, "I'm very conscious of how proud my father is of me."

THEN AGAIN, SO MUCH HAS CHANGED

There will always be fathers—and father figures like Mordecai—around to encourage and mentor their offspring. But much of what you may think you know about mentoring has changed in the not-too-distant past, and achieving success today requires tossing the old and embracing the new. For example . . .

> **ANCIENT WISDOM:**
> *The best mentors are ones assigned to you on the job.*
> **MODERN TRUTH:**
> *Glean all you can from these mentors, but find your own as well.*

Chances are, your firm offers some kind of formal mentoring program—71 percent of Fortune 500 and private companies do, according to a recent survey by the American Society for Training and Development.

At PricewaterhouseCoopers, for example, new hires are assigned a coach or mentor the first day they show up for work. The two have regular meetings and conversation, and the coach has input into evaluations and areas for skills growth, plus works on helping the new employee develop an annual personal plan.

Do these programs work? Two-thirds of female executives polled by Deloitte & Touche agree that they do and say that their most important professional relationship was with someone who had been assigned to them in a work-related setting.

Other studies show that formal mentoring programs work best when you're just starting with a new company or division. Then, once you've learned the ropes, you can seek out your own mentors. Formal mentoring programs can also be advantageous to women who feel intimidated about seeking out mentors on their own.

But there are downsides to formal mentoring programs. For starters, these programs often take a "shotgun" approach to matching mentors and protégés. That means you could get stuck with an incompatible or ineffective mentor which, in turn, could ruin your relationship or chances for promotion.

"Mentoring is such a popular human resources concept that employees in lots of companies are required to take on protégés whether they like it or not," says Nick A. Corcodilos, author of *Ask the Headhunter*. "But most mentoring programs I've seen, though born of good intentions, result in little more than awkward lunch meetings, because you can't really dictate how or whether two people will get along. Don't get me wrong: there are some very successful programs out there, but they're few and far between. The problem, I believe, is that too many of these programs are institutionally controlled rather than freewheeling."

Formal programs may not offer the results you're seeking, either. In one study comparing formal versus informal mentoring programs, protégés in informal mentorships reported more career-related support from their mentors and were earning higher salaries than those in formal programs.

ANCIENT WISDOM:
Wait for people to take you under their wing.
MODERN TRUTH:
Find someone's wings to grab onto.

In the palace, Hegai, the king's eunuch, was in charge of over-seeing all the young virgins in the king's harem. But lucky for Esther, he took a special liking to her—and, in effect, became her mentor.

"In the real world, mentors don't go out mentee hunting. Mentors want to associate with winners, with rising stars, so that some of the stardust will brush off on them," says Wellington.

The trick, then, is to find your own mentor. But first you need to figure out what you need, what you're looking for, and where your weaknesses lie. That way, you can hitch yourself to people who have the knowledge and know-how to make you stronger, more credible, and ultimately, more successful. So, do some soul searching.

Once you know what you need, your search begins—and that will require making a list of individuals who have the talent to ful-fill those needs. Who to put on your list? Consider people in your organization who possess the skills you want to acquire—or those you'd most like to emulate. Think back two or three assignments and recall people you admired, respected, and learned something from. Also, pay attention to things like who's most effective at meetings, who shines at motivating their staff, who gets the most respect from colleagues—and so on. Finally, decide if you need someone with skills different from your own or someone whose skills are similar to yours, but who has climbed farther up the ladder and might be willing to show you the way.

That's how Andrea Jung, president and CEO of Avon, found her mentor. After graduating magna cum laude from an Ivy League university, Jung planned to work a couple of years, then go to law school. At a college career fair, she was recruited by Bloomingdale's as a buyer. There, Jung admired, studied, be-friended and eventually convinced Karen Vass, the company's first

female vice president, to be her mentor. Vass was confident, articulate, and aggressive—the perfect role model to help Jung combat
what she called her "childhood Asian submissiveness." With Vass's
help, Jung climbed the ladder at Bloomingdale's—from Merchandising Manager to Vice President of Intimate Apparel.

Later, when Vass was recruited by I. Magnin to be that department store's first-ever female CEO, Jung was tapped to tag along.
"I think it's critical that you're working for a person who is committed to advancing your career," Jung said in an interview with
Goldsea, the Asian American Supersite (www.goldsea.com).

During her five-year tenure at I. Magnin, Jung scaled the
ranks from General Merchandise Manager to Senior Vice President, before she was wooed away by Neiman Marcus to be their
Executive Vice President of Merchandising. Two years later, she
landed at Avon, where she quickly rose from President of Product
Marketing for the U.S. to President and CEO.

After making your list of potential mentors—then what?
Taking a straightforward approach—by coming right out and
asking someone to be your mentor—is certainly one alternative.
But for most women, doing so feels awkward—plus there's always
that fear of rejection. Besides, many mentors like to believe that
they discovered *you*.

A better approach, then, is to do a little detective work. Get
more information about the potential mentors on your list by
talking to people who work closely with them or know them best.
Find out what projects they are working on—or what committees they serve on—and see what you can do to sign on. What do
they do outside the office? Are they members of nonprofits, or do
they sit on boards or organizations you can join to increase your
visibility around them?

When you're ready to approach your would-be mentor, Wellington advises making your pitch at an office event or social occasion. "If such a moment doesn't occur, you might arrange a meeting, or one of your network friends might help set one up," she says. "Even a cold call at the person's office door at the right moment can work in your favor."

And what to say once you're face-to-face with a potential mentor? Subtle (and sincere) flattery works best. "Tell that person what you admire about him or her, and ask whether he or she can tell you how to develop the same qualities," advises Linda Srere, president and CEO of giant ad agency Y & R New York. Even busy executives are often willing to help. "You'd be surprised at how rarely I say no to young people who want help or advice," Srere adds. "People at my level understand the importance of doing this."

Once you've broken the ice, work on connecting and clicking with that person over time and let your relationship evolve. Above all, keep in mind that the best mentoring relationships are mutually beneficial. So, make definite plans to contribute to the partnership.

ANCIENT WISDOM:
The best mentors are those who work inside your company.
MODERN TRUTH:
Mentors outside the company can offer a different perspective.

Hegai was the ideal mentor for Esther. He knew the palace culture inside out. And, as Carol M. Bechtel notes in her book *Interpretation: A Bible Commentary for Teaching and Preaching*, "Who would

ROYAL ADVICE

For the past three years, I've been working "in the trenches" as a line manager for a manufacturing company. Now I've been promoted to an executive-level position, and I need a mentor to show me the ropes. I have a prospect in mind, but I feel awkward asking him to be my mentor. Any suggestions?

Studies show that the best mentoring relationships are those that develop and evolve on their own. For this reason, we recommend putting yourself in a position that allows this to happen. Invite the person you have in mind to lunch. Tell him you'd like his input about a couple of projects you're working on. Call or e-mail your prospective mentor to ask advice about a particular problem you're struggling with. To further increase the amount of contact you have with your would-be mentor, ask to be appointed to a committee he chairs, or offer to pitch in with a pet project he's working on. Then see what happens. These strategies not only represent a more subtle approach, they also allow you to test the waters and see if pairing up with a certain person would be a good fit.

be more familiar with the king's most intimate preferences than Hegai, the keeper of Ahasuerus's harem?" Indeed, sharing this information with his protégé gave Esther a decisive edge when her turn arrived to "try out" for the part of queen.

One of the most persuasive arguments for finding a mentor

inside your "palace" comes from Ellen Snee and Jan Shubert, President and Vice President, respectively, of Fine Line Consulting. This Newton, Massachusetts, firm is dedicated to the advancement of female corporate leaders. It works with senior- and middle-management women in Fortune 100 and Fortune 500 companies to help them promote their efforts, tackle work obstacles, and navigate internal politics.

Not surprisingly, Fine Line encourages its clients to find effective mentors. "When companies seek to hire new talent, managers and other decision makers typically reach out for people they know," says Snee. "But women often haven't figured out how to be known."

Adds Shubert, "When doling out promotions, companies often consider three men and one woman for an open position. All of the candidates may be equally talented, but the woman stands alone and often doesn't know anyone in the higher ranks who could speak on her behalf."

For these reasons, Fine Line advises women to seek inside sponsors who can act as advocates when promotions roll around. "Women need someone who can say to them and a larger audience, 'Good job, brilliant work, keep it up!'" says Shubert.

Carly Fiorina, chair and CEO of Hewlett Packard—and *Fortune* magazine's number one pick as the most powerful businesswoman in America for five years running, agrees. "Nobody accomplishes any great things alone. I've been helped every step of the way by many people—including immediate bosses and my boss's boss—who believed in me."

Of course, your search for a mentor need not be an "inside job." People outside your organization can be equally effective. In Esther's case, for example, Mordecai served as her mentor outside the palace. Through messengers, he kept her abreast of all that was going on in and around Susa, and as problems arose, he offered her valuable advice.

Catalyst's Sheila Wellington found equally valuable advice from an outside mentor. She began her career working for a community health center in New Haven, Connecticut, rising through the ranks to deputy director. But when her boss decided to move on, it never occurred to Wellington that she should apply for the job. "It never would have without the encouragement of a mentor—a former professor who not only advised me to go for it but showed me how to do it," she says. "It was, for me, a critical point. It really caused me to stop and think."

Wellington snagged the directorship. Then, years later, after taking on the challenge of turning around a scandal-ridden mental hospital, her appointment came under fire—"because I was a woman and because I was not a psychiatrist," she reports. "Once again, the same mentor came to my defense and helped silence my critics."

Wellington went on to become the first female secretary of Yale University before making the move to head up Catalyst.

As Wellington's story illustrates, often the best mentors are found outside your workplace. And this may be particularly true in companies that don't offer formal mentoring programs, in situations where few women occupy executive suites, and/or where female-friendly mentors are scarce. As Ronna Lichtenberg points out in her book *It's Not Business, It's Personal,* "Too often, women target the few females at the top of their organization who are already overwhelmed by requests to mentor someone."

Where to look outside your organization for a mentor? Professional organizations you belong to are an excellent place to start. Other fertile grounds include Chambers of Commerce, alumni associations, community boards you serve on, and networking groups you're a part of.

Yet another option: cyberspace. In recent years, online mentoring opportunities have flourished, with thousands of women logging on to join small, highly focused discussion groups offering career advice, strategies for breaking through the glass ceiling, job transition advice, and tips on work/family balance. There are definite advantages to "e-mentoring," "telementoring," or "virtual mentoring." For starters, you have immediate access to tremendous amounts of information, plus it's available 24/7. The relative anonymity of the Internet enables you to discuss sensitive issues or personal on-the-job problems without feeling uncomfortable as you might with face-to-face contact. What's more, chat rooms and Web pages that focus on mentoring offer different perspectives from online mentors with a variety of backgrounds.

Where to click? SCORE (www.score.org), which stands for Service Corp. of Retired Executives, matches protégés with retired businesspeople who were successful in their various careers. Global Mecca (www.globalmecca.com) provides career coaching for African-American professionals. At iVillage (www.ivillage.com/work), you'll find a wealth of chat rooms and message boards filled with would-be mentors representing every imaginable profession. And if you're currently pursuing a degree in engineering, science, technology, or mathematics, check out MentorNet (www.mentornet.net), where you can sign up for e-mail mentoring from established professionals.

ANCIENT WISDOM:
Males make better mentors for females.
MODERN TRUTH:
You need both male and female mentors.

When looking for a mentor, does gender matter? Some researchers believe it does, and that your choice should depend on what you're looking for in the relationship.

Female mentors appear to be better role models, but male mentors may be better at leading the way to the top of the corporate ladder. That's the conclusion of a recent Pennsylvania State University study that involved 200 protégés—all graduate students, ranging in age from 20 to 57. Specifically, researchers surveyed 115 men and 85 women, who rated 139 male and 61 female mentors from many industries on a variety of factors.

Women's strengths? In Esther's case, she had a bevy of maids-in-waiting at her beck and call. Once crowned, she relied heavily on the support and advice of these women as she assumed her new duties. And later, when times got tough, these women offered her the emotional support she needed to make wise decisions.

In essence, women excel at offering personal support, friendship, acceptance, counseling, and role modeling. With women guiding you, it's usually more about commitment and chemistry with the emphasis on personal growth and development rather than about promotions.

Two years after launching The Publicity Hound, a Saukville, Wisconsin, media relations and employee retention consultancy, owner Joan Stewart realized she needed a mentor to help her grow her business. "I discovered that the Milwaukee Women's Business Initiative, Inc., a nonprofit that aids business owners, sponsored a mentoring program that matches more seasoned female entrepreneurs with those who are a bit newer to the game," she says.

Stewart attended a meeting where she heard Cheryl Muskus speak. "I knew right away that she'd be the perfect mentor for me. She was strong in the areas that I was weak," Stewart says. "When

I found out that she had been assigned to someone else, I immediately got on the phone and told them, 'I need to have this woman as my mentor. I'll do whatever it takes.'"

The pair's formal arrangement has since ended, but their friendship endures. Muskus, an accounting software consultant based in Muskego, Wisconsin, helped Stewart set up business systems in financial and information management. Even more valuable, she assured Stewart she was not alone.

"Cheryl would listen to my problems and say, 'Joan, the questions that you are struggling with are problems that most business owners struggle with. You are not unique. You are not crazy. You are not incompetent.'"

Her mentor also forced Stewart to look within to find answers to questions and to form her own opinions. "She didn't want me to live by her code of ethics," Stewart says. "She forced me to think about where I was going, rather than follow someone else's path."

By nature, female mentors also tend to be warmer and more approachable, as well as more willing to share pieces of themselves. Naturally, female mentors are better at offering advice on bridging the divide that often exists between men and women in the workplace. After all, they've been in the trenches; they know how to play the game.

With female mentors, there is no danger of sexual harassment; sexual undercurrents are also nonexistent. Granted, as Joan Jeruchim and Pat Shapiro, coauthors of *Women, Mentors, and Success*, note, female mentors often "lack the power to link their protégés to important people or to sponsor them for key committees or projects." Nevertheless, you can generally count on more bonding, nurturing, and confidence-building with a female mentor.

This story, adapted from Arthur Gordon's book *A Touch of Wonder*, illustrates the advantages of choosing a female mentor . . .

In the early years of the 20th century, some of the most talented writers at the University of Wisconsin gathered into two groups. The male group called themselves the Stranglers, due to their ruthless criticism of each other's work.

Indeed, they were merciless with one another. They dissected the most minute literary expression into a hundred pieces. They were heartless, tough, even mean in their criticism.

The women called their group the Wranglers, but they operated very differently. Their criticism was much softer, more positive, more encouraging. Sometimes there was almost no criticism at all. Every effort, even the most feeble one, was encouraged.

Twenty years later, an alumnus of the university was doing an exhaustive study of his classmates' careers when he noticed a vast difference in the literary accomplishments of the Stranglers as opposed to the Wranglers. Not one of the Stranglers had forged a successful literary career. From the Wranglers, however, had come six or more successful writers, some of them nationally renown. One shining example: Marjorie Kinnan Rawlings, a 1918 graduate, who had earned a national reputation with her Pulitzer Prize-winning novel, *The Yearling*.

The male advantage? In Esther's case, it was Hegai who was probably the most influential in helping her become queen. After all, he was privy to the king's likes and dislikes and was able to tip Esther off accordingly. As a rule of thumb, the same holds true today. In terms of career development—which involves functions such as sponsorship, protection, providing challenging assignments, exposure, and visibility—both male and female protégés in the Penn State study said they received greater assistance from male mentors. Study authors John S. Sosik, Ph.D., and Veronica M. Godshalk, Ph.D., agree that much of this might be associated with stereotypes of men and women in the corporate world. "Both men and women perceive men as possessing more and different forms of power than women," Godshalk confirms. "Within traditional male-dominated organizations, both male and female protégés may shy away from female mentors when seeking career development functions leading to promotions."

In fact, in their study, male mentors emerged especially effective at helping female protégés. "Among other things, male mentors can help female protégés overcome discriminating barriers in place at traditional organizations," says Sosik. They may also be better positioned to make critical introductions for you, as Pamela Thomas-Graham's story illustrates.

At age 32, this Harvard business school graduate became the first African-American woman to make partner at the prestigious management consulting firm McKinsey & Company. Today, as an executive vice president of NBC and president and CEO of CNBC.com, she is the highest-ranking woman executive running a division at NBC. "You can't have a successful career without mentors," she says.

In fact, Thomas-Graham credits one of her male mentors with helping her land the NBC job. As a partner in retail and media practice at McKinsey, one of her specialties was helping clients build Internet businesses. Thus, in 1999, when she expressed an interest in moving on, her mentor arranged a meeting for Thomas-Graham with General Electric Chairman Jack Welch.

GE, which owns NBC and CNBC.com, seemed a good fit for Thomas-Graham, and she and Welch clicked. Indeed, as luck would have it, when the two met, Welch was already looking at expanding CNBC.com from a promotional tool for the CNBC cable channel to a full-service financial site. Welch soon made Thomas-Graham an offer, and she was thrilled with the opportunity to head the site.

In many surveys, however, a mentor's gender is not an issue. More important is that the chemistry works and that you and your mentor work well together toward the same goals.

ANCIENT WISDOM:
*Mentors should be higher up the ladder
than you are.*
MODERN TRUTH:
*Someone on your level, even below it, may have
plenty to offer.*

Conventional wisdom says that mentors should have seniority over you. After all, someone who's already learned the ropes and has more experience than you do is certain to give you better advice—right? "These mentors can prepare you for higher levels of responsibility by giving you a sneak preview of what it means to have power—removing some of the mystery," says Claire Farley, president of Texaco's North American oil and gas exploration unit. "And by sharing their own experiences with you and giving you objective criticism and support, mentors really help you stretch."

But the most effective mentors don't necessarily have to

have seniority on you. Look at Esther! As queen of Persia, she had seniority over every one of her mentors—Hegai, her maids-in-waiting, even her cousin Mordecai. Lourdes Townsend also discovered this to be true when recently offered a promotion to international marketing manager at Stride Rite. Accepting the position meant interrupting her pursuit of her MBA, so Townsend knew she would need a mentor.

A colleague she turned to for advice recommended a program run by WOMEN Unlimited, Inc., a New York City–based career development company for women only. The program paired Townsend with a senior executive outside of Stride Rite who would be her mentor for a year. It also exposed her to 20 peers-as-mentors who met at monthly workshops and who, ultimately, taught Townsend more than either her MBA classes or her formal mentor would.

"These were all smart, ambitious women from various companies in the Boston area," Townsend says. "I never thought about learning from someone on my own level. I always looked two to three levels above me and wondered what I had to do to get there. But the people who have the best solutions to the problems I face are often the people facing those problems themselves."

Another approach to mentoring that is growing in popularity entails organizations shifting into reverse. Seasoned executives are still paired with rookies, but not for reasons you'd think. "Many companies are asking tech-savvy new hires to teach the 'old dogs' new tricks," says Matt Starcevich, CEO of the Center for Coaching and Mentoring in Bartlesville, Oklahoma.

In fact, a recent study he conducted found that 41 percent of the companies surveyed were using reverse mentoring to spread technical expertise, and 26 percent relied on younger staff members to gain a more youthful perspective.

And these are big-name companies—like Texas Instruments, Tyco International, and even General Electric, where former CEO Jack Welch ordered 500 of his top managers to find workers who were well versed in the Internet and tap into their expertise. Welch himself chose a mentor and blocked off time to learn about everything from Internet bookmarks to competitors' Web sites.

"Reverse mentoring can provide substantial benefits for an organization," says Starcevich. "Executives are beginning to realize that knowledge isn't a one-way street, and that it's in everyone's best interest to share expertise."

ANCIENT WISDOM:
One or two mentors are all you need in your career.
MODERN TRUTH:
The more, the merrier.

Don't expect to have the same mentor your entire career—the average mentoring relationship lasts five years, studies show. But do expect to have mentors throughout your career, depending on where you are, where you're headed, and what your greatest needs are at the time.

In fact, 85 percent of the executive women polled by Deloitte & Touche said that at least three or more individuals influenced their personal and professional development.

Wellington believes that women should build a mentor base and approach this task as if they were building a board of directors for a company. "Create a panel of many levels of experience, in a wide range of areas, inside and outside your company," she says. "That way, you can get the inside dope from one person, style tips from another, feedback from the third, and so on. It's a win-win situation and you'll get advice on a wide range of career path options, more opinions, and a broader perspective. And you won't exhaust anyone in the process."

Mary S. Spaeth, founder and CEO of Transmera AB in Sweden (AB is the equivalent of Inc. in the U.S.), agrees. She began her career as director of marketing and public relations for the Northwestern University Evanston Research Park, then moved up to executive vice president of ANGLE Technology LLC, based in Washington, D.C. Today, at the helm of her new start-up company, Spaeth works with municipal, regional, and national economic development, particularly in the technology commercialization arena—supporting the creation of new business from university research through effective "incubation." Currently, she is project leader for a new bioscience initiative for the Stockholm region. She is also working on a pre-study for a new science park in St. Petersburg, Russia, plus teaches entrepreneurship and business development at Linkoping University in Sweden.

"My mentors have come in many forms and from all levels," she says. "And all have taught me something valuable." One former mentor in Chicago, for example, told Spaeth she didn't listen well enough. "Since moving to Sweden, I've had to learn the language, and that's helped me listen more," she laughs.

In Sweden, Spaeth has also learned to ask for help without feeling weak. "Here my mentors have been local bankers and a CEO of a company located on the Science Park here whom I met five years ago when he came to Chicago to look for a headquarters for his company. There's Peter, a man who brought books to me to read and listened to me struggle through Swedish newspapers week after week. There's Ola, who believed in my talent and expertise enough to support my application to lead this new project in Stockholm. There's Helena, the science park secretary who tells me when she doesn't like things I do—and why—and then we laugh together. And it's all of the Swedish women—mothers, business professionals, professors, and others—whose strength and persona are unmatched, to my mind, anywhere else on the globe."

The bottom line is, mentoring has many faces . . .

For instance, there are job-specific mentors. These are folks—typically at your level or just above it—who help you learn the ropes in a new job. This kind of mentor can help you adjust to your new culture, interpret feedback and directions from your new boss, and help you clear hurdles associated with being the "new kid on the block."

On the flip side, there are career-specific mentors, who not only help you plot long-term goals but assist in creating a road map for you to reach your aspirations. Since these mentors must be able to provide feedback on the skills you'll need to acquire to reach the next level, they are almost always higher up in an organization than you are.

There are also situational mentors—people you turn to for advice when handling a problem, or folks you depend on to help you brainstorm ideas. This type of mentor can be found anywhere inside or outside of an organization. It can be your boss, a colleague, a parent, a best friend—even a group of "angels."

Consider Antoinette Bruno's story. This CEO of StarChefs, a struggling dot-com serving the restaurant industry, met her mentors—8 Wings, a group of angel investors who serve as business advisors to women-led companies—at a venture-capital networking event. "She was a success waiting to happen," says 8 Wings partner Sharon Whiteley.

Her mentors helped Bruno refocus her company from a restaurant supply business to a hiring and training site for restaurateurs—an industry that employs more than 17 million people nationally but has an average annual employee turnover rate of 120 percent. "Our site already had a jobs board, but we just weren't focusing on it," says Bruno. "8 Wings helped me to see what was staring right at me."

Bruno's mentors encouraged her to partner with another company to develop restaurant-training programs modeled after video games. Today, StarChefs makes money from selling these programs as well as ad space on its job board, and business these days is brisk. In fact, StarChefs.com receives a whopping ten million hits per month and has captured "Best of the Web" awards from *USA Today*, U.S. News Online, Brill's Content, and Lycos.

According to Jeruchim and Shapiro, there are even symbolic mentors—or people (mostly women) who inspire us. A major role model in Elizabeth Dole's life, for example, was her grandmother, "Mom Cathey," who lived to be nearly one hundred years old. "She practiced what she preached and lived her life for others," Dole writes in *Finding God at Harvard*. "I cannot remember an unkind word escaping her lips in all the years that I knew her, or an ungracious deed marring her path. I wanted to be like Mom Cathey. In many ways, she was my Mordecai."

Symbolic mentors, Jeruchim and Shapiro add, can even be mythical figures (like Athena), historical figures (like Joan of Arc), pioneers (like Amelia Earhart), biblical heroines (like Queen Esther!), or someone prominent you admire in your professional today.

"When a writer we know couldn't find a mentor, she used a well-known writer whom she admired, as a symbolic mentor," the authors explain. "She told us, 'I had never met her, but she haunted me and influenced my career. First it was her in-depth medical stories for the Sunday magazine, then her features in the nationals, and the latest, a book. What next? I read her articles with envy and awe. She frustrated me yet spurred me on. If she could write so well, so could I. She was my ideal, my nemesis, my mentor in fantasy.'"

Of course, you don't have to connect with just one mentor at a time. As Shirley Peddy points out in *The Art of Mentoring*, "Often one person can give you one kind of advice, and someone else can help in another way."

Neither should you overlook what Peddy calls "Mentoring Moments"—which she describes as "those small bits of advice you can garner here and there from experienced professionals."

ANCIENT WISDOM:
The best mentors are people you have plenty in common with.
MODERN TRUTH:
Often the best match is a mismatch.

Finding a mentor with a different background or path to success than yours almost always makes for a more enriching experience. Contrasting personality types can be advantageous as well, in that your mentor can provide guidance where you need it most.

"If you're matched with someone who's like you, the potential for discovery is negated," says Gayle Holmes, founder, president, and CEO of Menttium Corporation, a Minnesota-based mentoring service that matches mentors and mentees from different companies in six cities. "You should always pair with someone who, by her very nature, will challenge you."

The best mentors are also people you don't know very well. Otherwise, you might not be as honest with them. The point of mentoring is to provide you with constructive feedback, and to push you into areas beyond your comfort zone. Then you *really* learn something.

Can your boss be your mentor? Possibly. After all a boss's job entails guiding you, challenging you, coaching you, and developing you. And many bosses will do all they can to help you shine, since your successes make them look good as well.

But there's a flip side to consider. Bringing up personal issues with someone who's responsible for directing and evaluating you doesn't make for good mentoring. With a mentor, you should feel free to share failures. That way, the two of you can figure out what went wrong and how to succeed the next time. But if you do this with a boss, it could affect your next performance review—and your salary.

ANCIENT WISDOM:
Hanging in there with a bad mentor is smarter than walking away—and possibly jeopardizing your career.

MODERN TRUTH:
In most cases, "divorcing" a mentor is a smarter move.

Throughout her ordeal, Esther was fortunate enough to maintain positive relationships with her entire support group. But as the plot of her story thickened—and with all the drama going on in the palace—there were plenty of opportunities for any one of her mentors to turn against her. Wisely, Esther continued to cultivate these relationships and keep her support network intact.

Mentoring relationships can be as fragile as any other personal relationship you enter into. Sometimes personalities clash, or the right chemistry just isn't there. Other times, relationships sour when expectations aren't met or when mentor-mentees outgrow one another.

In fact, in one recent study, University of Georgia psychologist Lillian Eby, Ph.D., found that over half of the 242 protégés she surveyed reported at least one negative mentoring experience in their careers. "We were surprised that it was that common," she says.

Most of the pitfalls the subjects in this study encountered fell into two categories. "Some had to do with a poor fit between the mentor and protégé, a mismatch in people's personalities, values, or work styles," Eby reports. "Others had to do with mentors who were not technically or interpersonally skilled or who neglected the protégé."

Then there was a third category, which Eby found "a bit more shocking," that dealt with mentors who engage in antisocial behaviors with protégés. "They manipulated their protégé for personal gain," she explains. "Or they deceived their protégé or wielded power inappropriately."

"The worst advice I ever got was, 'Stick with me, babe!'—and it came from a male mentor who treated me like a jewel locked in a closet," says Kathy Biro, cofounder and vice chairman of Digitas, a marketing and technical services firm. "I could always feel the imprint of his foot as he stepped on my back to climb that ladder."

Fortunately, studies show that cases like these are far less common than problems related to mismatch or neglect.

What to do if *your* relationship with a mentor turns dysfunctional? Don't hesitate to end it. After all, channeling energy into a negative or difficult relationship is a waste of time for both of you—time that could be spent in far more productive ways.

Other legitimate reasons to move on? When you need skills

you don't think your mentor can provide . . . when your mentor no longer has sufficient time to spend with you . . . or when a mentor micromanages you by telling you how to do your job or by offering solutions or making decisions for you without your input.

Biro's advice? "Seek out mentors who are motivated by your best interests, not theirs."

Of course, your mentor may be reluctant to let you go. "In that case, it's important to create the maneuver with delicacy. You might not even have to say you're ending the relationship; you can just let it wither naturally," says Wellington.

Keep in mind, though, that while there may be many legitimate reasons for ending a relationship with a mentor, think twice before making such a move if your only beef is "He's pushing me too hard," or "She's so critical." According to Candice Carpenter, cofounder and former CEO of iVillage, you may have lucked out by landing what she calls a "radical mentor." And it could be the best thing that could ever happen to you—and your career.

Radical mentors, she explains, "move people along faster than they want to go. It's not natural for people to grow as fast as you need them to. People don't grow if you're soft with them. You catapult people forward by being extremely blunt."

In today's fast-paced and constantly changing business environment, Carpenter is convinced that it is this kind of mentoring women need most. "People have a much greater capacity for growth than they get credit for," she says. "Once you get your first taste of being really challenged, you want to be challenged more."

YOUR ROLE AS A MENTEE

Successful mentor-mentee relationships are *always* reciprocal. That means you must assume certain responsibilities to make the relationship work. To do your part—and enter into a

♔
ROYAL ADVICE

I've learned so much from my mentor over the years. Now that the focus of my job has changed, however, she doesn't have the expertise I need—and she's even been giving me some bad advice. Unfortunately, she's above me in the chain of command. How can I put an end to this obsolete relationship without jeopardizing my chances of moving up?

The most effective mentoring relationships are designed to achieve specific goals. Then, once those goals have been met, the relationship should end. Savvy mentors know this—and chances are, yours may realize she's no longer as effective at helping you. In fact, she may be waiting for you to initiate the break, for fear of letting *you* down. If you suspect this may be the case, take the direct approach by telling your mentor that your needs have changed, by thanking her profusely for her years of support, and by promising to keep in touch.

relationship with the right mindset—we advise abiding by these four golden rules.

1. Your mentor's time is valuable; don't monopolize it. Marty Brounstein, author of *Coaching and Mentoring for Dummies*, cautions against looking to your mentor as "an all-knowing, all-telling, come-to-the-rescue savior." A mentor's role, after all, is not to tell you how to do your job. Nor does it involve making deci-

sions or solving problems for you without your input. Rather, a mentor is there to counsel and guide you into thinking for yourself and finding your own solutions. And all of this should occur on his or her timetable.

2. Be prepared to give something back. Anyone who is willing to offer guidance, advice, and time is going to expect something in return. Usually, that something is either loyalty or gratitude. There are many powerful words in the English language, but don't overlook the two most powerful: "Thank you."

3. You must be willing to pay your dues. Jeruchim and Shapiro point out, "Some mentors may want you to work long hours on one of their projects in return for their teaching, coaching, and support. So, think hard—beforehand—about whether you're willing to pay your dues for the opportunity to work with them."

4. Have realistic expectations. "You can't expect a mentoring relationship to be wonderful all the time," says Eby. "Mentors have lives. Mentors have careers. They may not be able to allocate the time necessary to you. They may not always look out for your best interest. It's important for both parties to realize that, like any relationship, mentoring relationships are going to have their ups and downs."

The good news is, protégés aren't the only ones to reap rewards in successful mentoring relationships. Studies show mentors gain leadership practice, personal satisfaction, and increased networking opportunities. As teachers, mentors keep themselves sharp. And by setting good examples for their protégés, mentors often improve their own performances to boot! ♛

3

IT PAYS TO KNOW
THE PALACE GOSSIP

*O*ne day, Mordecai was sitting at the palace gate—a place
*where all the business and legal decisions of the kingdom
were made. There, he overheard two of the king's officers
plotting to assassinate the king . . .*

Bingthan and Teresh, two of the king's officials from
those who guarded the door, became angry and sought
to lay hands on King Ahasuerus.
—Esther 2:21

*Mordecai was alarmed at overhearing the two men plotting
their conspiracy against the king and immediately sent word to
Esther to tell her what he had learned. Esther, in turn, went to her
husband to tell the unsuspecting king of the assassination plot. With
Esther's warning, her loyalty and credibility soared in the king's eyes.*

And when the report was investigated and found to be
true, the two officials were hanged on a gallows. All this
was recorded in the book of the annals in the presence of
the king.
—Esther 2:21–23

Pssst! Have you heard the latest? Today, as in biblical times,
gossip can offer enormous benefits. Handled constructively in

the workplace, it can be used to enhance your reputation, increase your visibility, and provide you with the kind of information you need to make smart career moves. It can help you get closer to influential people, and to distance yourself from those who might undermine—or interfere with—your success. The grapevine can also tune you into people's hot buttons—plus help you pow-wow with peers, bond with bosses, and even make friends of enemies.

Gossip can even help you get ahead. "Through the grapevine, you can find out valuable information about your boss's likes and dislikes," reveals Marilyn Moats Kennedy, author of *Office Politics: Serving Power/Wielding Clout.* "You may even learn the fate of your predecessor!"

That's exactly how Esther used gossip to her advantage. Through the grapevine, she learned that King Ahasuerus was seeking a queen who would be "better than Vashti." And by snooping around the palace, she was able to uncover details about how and why her predecessor had been banished.

To Esther, Vashti's story was a crystal clear example of how *not* to do things if she intended to hang on to her title. Armed with this knowledge, she was also able to develop and shape her own behavior so as to be pleasing to her husband and boss, the king.

How to use gossip to *your* advantage? Here's the scoop . . .

TAPPING INTO THE OFFICE GRAPEVINE

Julia, a senior manager in the banking industry, says she has no use for gossip. "It's toxic, and it's an occupational hazard," she believes. "To do my job, I really don't need to know everyone's personal secrets."

For this reason, Julia never stops to chitchat in the hallway or at the watercooler. And she rarely "does lunch" or joins colleagues after work.

"Big mistake," says career coach Marcia Greene. Many workers like Julia assume that the lion's share of gossip that travels around most offices is about personal matters. But according to a recent poll of 1,000 top U.S. companies, 40 percent of executives said that watercooler discussions typically focus on business-related matters—who's getting hired, fired, or promoted, for example. Which means that if you're not tuned into the office grapevine, you could miss out on valuable inside information.

The wicked Haman, you'll soon discover, ignored the grape-vine and paid dearly for it. "Haman was so busy touting his power and influence around town that he failed to listen to the rumbling that would eventually undo him," acknowledges Dianna Booher in her book *The Esther Effect*.

Certainly, gossip *can* be toxic. But more often than not, it's informative. In fact, used effectively, the grapevine can be an important tool in managing your career. "When you're up to date about your firm's future, you can respond accordingly," says Greene. "And that can mean the difference between moving up the ladder or out the door."

Andrea's story is a perfect example. Eight months ago, this vice president at an insurance company in the Northeast got wind that her firm would soon be taken over by a larger company. "Fortunately, I had a couple of high-level contacts there and was able to get the inside scoop on whose positions were most likely to be at risk," she says. "Unfortunately, mine was one of them, but I also found out who the new decision-makers (in my firm) would be following the merge, and that enabled me to spend the next few months subtly aligning myself with them. Meanwhile, I

also updated my résumé and put some feelers out for a new job—
just in case."

Andrea's strategy worked. After the merger, her position *was*
eliminated—but instead of being laid off, she managed to snag a
promotion.

By keeping your ear to the ground, you can also avoid getting politically blindsided. "Knowledge makes you powerful,"
agrees Kennedy. "If you know about a crisis (or even an opportunity) in advance, you can figure out how it may affect you, and
you can plan a response. If you're not wired in, you simply react
after the fact."

"Last year, my mentor told me in confidence that our company was getting ready to do some major downsizing and that
roughly half of the middle management staff would be laid off,"
says Charlotte, who works in middle management for a food service company. "I knew I had a good chance of surviving the cut,
but I also knew my responsibilities would double, and I was
already working 12-hour days. So I did some major networking
and managed to make a quick lateral move to another company."

In retrospect, Charlotte thinks hers was a smart move. "Half
of my former colleagues got laid off and are looking for jobs. And
the ones who stayed are totally burned out."

"Gossip is the only thing that travels faster than the speed of
light," says Joel R. DeLuca, Ph.D., author of *Political Savvy: Systematic Approaches to Leadership behind the Scenes*. "To help your
career, you need to make sure you're part of the lightning rod that
catches that information."

How to make sure you meet the right people and hear all the
need-to-know news? "You gotta schmooze," says Greene. "To gain
access to insider information, you have to raise your visibility by
networking both inside and outside your company."

This entails occasionally dropping by colleagues' offices to chat, taking the initiative to invite others who are "in the loop" out to lunch, and making every effort to attend after-work get-togethers.

It also entails paying attention at networking events, business conferences, and such. "Figure out who's worth getting to know better, then introduce yourself, hand them a business card, and say you'd like to keep in touch," Greene advises. "Follow up with an e-mail and make plans to get together one-on-one. That way, you can ask, 'So what's new over at your office?' to get the scoop."

ENGINEERING POSITIVE GOSSIP ABOUT YOURSELF

Is it possible to initiate positive rumors about yourself that will ultimately work to your advantage? You bet it is! And Kathryn Hays' story offers excellent proof. Now a filmmaker, Hays began her career as a banker. "I was one of the youngest branch managers at a Texas-based bank, and the branch I was assigned to was in terrible shape," she recalls. "It had recently failed an audit, customer complaints were high, employee morale was low, and financially speaking, the bank itself ranked among the lowest in the district."

Charged with shaping things up, Hays decided that the only way she could meet that challenge would be to focus first on employee morale. "Instead of harping on people's weaknesses, I zeroed in on each individual's strengths," she says. "If someone excelled at customer service, they became Customer Service Supervisor. If someone else excelled at detailed bookkeeping, they became our Audit Specialist. While these titles didn't carry much weight outside our branch, the immediate result was greater employee confidence and a newly acquired sense of pride."

Within six months, Hays had turned things around. "The branch received excellent ratings at its next audit, sales and new accounts increased, and customer satisfaction surveys were glowing," she reports.

Then, one of Hays' supervisors changed banks and called her with a job offer to work her magic on one of his "problem" branches. That offer came with a hefty pay raise and guaranteed commissions on sales, so Hays agreed to make the leap. "The only fly in the ointment was that this particular branch was right across the street from where I was already working—and my predecessor had been demoted to assistant branch manager at that same branch. In fact, I was told that the employees were resentful of this personnel shuffle and had already sworn allegiance to the old branch manager—against any outside intruder."

None of this, however, deterred Hays, who loves a challenge. Instead, she decided to think of a way to win over her new employees before she took over as their new boss. Her solution? To engineer some good gossip about herself.

"Luckily, I had several customers who banked at both branches," she says. "So, I confided in a few by simply telling them that I had a reputation for being a tough, no-nonsense manager, who was fully capable of firing first and asking questions later. I told these customers that I could replace tellers and new account managers in a matter of days and wouldn't hesitate to do so if employees gave me any problems. After all, I explained, I didn't get the reputation of being a 'problem solver' for nothing."

A week later, Hays visited the branch across the street and "shopped" the tellers—taking notes, etc. and making sure everyone saw her. "The weekend before I was to take over as branch manager of the new bank, my new supervisor called me and asked, 'What the hell have you done to those people?'" reports Hays.

Obviously, word had spread that Hays was tough, mean, and ready to clean house. Rumor had it that she even had the backing of the entire company behind her. "Not only was the branch dreading my arrival, but the entire district was abuzz wondering just who the heck I was!" Hays laughs.

Day one at her new job, Hays called a meeting ("with the district manager there for extra support") to announce her goals, expectations, and strategies for getting the branch to the top. "I let everyone know that I was fair, would work hard to see them excel, and be supportive of their growth—but I would not tolerate irresponsible or destructive behaviors."

The outcome? Hays did eventually have to fire the demoted ex-branch manager—"primarily for her continued efforts to undermine me and sabotage my relationship with corporate headquarters. But the remaining employees became a wonderful team and, as before, I assigned them each a 'department' that they would head."

Within a year, Hays' new branch emerged one of the top ten branches in the state and achieved excellent ratings in audits and sales.

"The truth is, I *was* tough, but not as tough as my 'engineered' reputation," she says. "I believe that image forced my staff to decide to whom they would vow allegiance. In most cases, people will side with individuals whom they believe can lead and win. The ex-manager had already proved that although she could be their friend, she could not be a leader or a winner."

"Granted, I could have gone in there trying desperately to win them over with my charm and warm cookies—as most women are taught to do," she adds. "But surely they would have chewed me up and spit me out. So, sometimes a little engineered gossip is a good thing!"

Indeed, the beauty of gossip is that it allows you to be your own P.R. agent. After all, since it's inevitable that coworkers will talk about you anyway, you can make sure that what's being said about you works in your favor by . . .

Being efficient. "Send cordial thank-you notes, return phone calls and e-mails promptly, and always be upbeat about yourself and your company—even if you're having a rotten day," advises author Sue Browder. "By staying optimistic, you create a 'halo' effect, wherein whenever coworkers talk about you, they mostly have good things to say."

Being nice to support staff. Esther reaped huge benefits by befriending her maids-in-waiting and the king's eunuchs. You can do the same by building mutually supportive relationships with janitors, secretaries, and administrative assistants in your office. Susan RoAne, a former San Francisco elementary school teacher and author of *The Secrets of Savvy Networking*, agrees. "Often the little people can do the most for you—and I speak from personal experience. One day, the school secretary where I worked told me the program that funded my job was about to be cut. Thanks to that piece of intelligence, I was able to launch a successful campaign to keep the program—and my position."

"These folks are very important in the grapevine, and they have informal, if not formal, power," acknowledges Kennedy. "Many young workers assume secretaries—because they are in support jobs—don't have power, but this is wrong. They have tremendous influence with their bosses, and this is particularly true of executive secretaries. If a secretary speaks highly of you to a vice president, her comments will be taken seriously. If she speaks slightingly of you, or worse, mentions a specific indiscretion, it can be very damaging. The rule is that nobody in your work environment can be ignored or offended—ever."

Singing others' praises. Anytime your colleagues do well, praise them not only to their faces, but also behind their backs, Browder suggests. Examples: "Did you hear Rhonda got a paper published?" or "Have you seen that glowing thank-you note Peter got from one of his clients?" By repeating only good news about others, you establish a loyal network, Browder adds. "When friends in other companies hear about great job openings, you'll be the first person they call. And if anyone tries to bad-mouth you behind your back, you'll have so many supporters that someone will inevitably spring to your defense and squelch any rumors before they begin."

Learning to gossip like a man. Think men don't gossip? Think again! In recent studies, researchers eavesdropped in restaurants and cafés and discovered that both sexes spend roughly the same amount of time gossiping. But while women are more likely to discuss the behavior of other people, men prefer to gossip about their own achievements.

Researchers also found gender differences in the motives behind gossiping. Women use gossip to bond and increase closeness, by telling stories to one another. Men, on the other hand, use gossip to build status, by trading tales of triumph.

Granted, many women are reluctant to boast about their achievements, but there are ways around that.

"When I recently won a prestigious award from a nonprofit agency I've worked with for years, all I had to do was show the statuette I received to my secretary and tell her how excited I was," says Robin Lewis-Carpenter, a senior vice president at a telecommunications company. "She insisted I display my award on the

ROYAL ADVICE

Someone in my office has been spreading gossip about me. I know who it is, but what's the best way to handle this? Should I confront her or just wait for the rumors to die down?

That depends. If it's relatively harmless gossip, you could play it cool by saying something like, "Is that what people are saying about me?" Then laugh. If *you* treat a rumor as ridiculous, gossipers around you will quickly see how ridiculous it is, too.

If the gossip is malicious, however, you should definitely confront the person who's spreading it. Do this privately and calmly. Causing a scene will only make the other person feel justified in spreading venom. Not to mention that if you fly off the handle, you give people something else to gossip about!

Do be firm, however, when you say, "What you've been saying about me isn't true, and I will not tolerate such malicious gossip being spread by you." Then wait for an apology and accept it graciously.

Above all, keep in mind that no matter how mean people may seem, almost everyone feels bad if they're confronted with actually hurting someone else. And they usually don't repeat their mistakes.

table outside my office, and in no time, the entire office was abuzz with the news."

Enlisting the help of a colleague to reenact the "Polish Generalissima's Paradigm." According to Harriet Rubin, author of *The Princess Machiavelli for Women* and *Soloing: Realizing Your Life Ambition*, here's how this strategy works: "Two women in the Polish military made a secret pact. They decided to help each other rise in the hierarchy. Whenever Magda went to a meeting, she'd be sure to work praise of Theresa into the discussion. Whenever Theresa wrote a report, she recommended Magda for new responsibilities. Before long, third parties were saying, 'I hear Theresa is brilliant' or 'Magda is being considered for X promotion.' Both rose in the hierarchy simultaneously!"

KNOWING WHEN TO QUIP— AND WHEN TO ZIP YOUR LIP

Heard through the grapevine about a merger taking place in your industry? Got the inside scoop on a big client your company is courting? By all means, share the news with your boss. By doing so, you'll be recognized as a savvy player. "And this is true even if the person you tell is already privy to the information," says Greene.

In fact, spilling information to your higher-ups is almost always a no-lose move. Esther did this when she heard about the guards' plot to assassinate the king. By passing on this juicy tidbit to her husband, she gained credibility and honor in the king's eyes.

"The best thing you can do on the job is to help your boss win," notes Ronna Lichtenberg, author of *Work Would Be Great if It Weren't for the People*. Indeed, Lauren, a senior buyer at a department store, scored major points with her boss by passing along a great word-of-mouth morsel. "When a friend at a rival store told me their advertising budget had been cut in half until the end of the fiscal year, I told my boss. She immediately increased our ads for the next few months, and sales figures doubled. A year later, when my boss was offered a better job at another store, she insisted on taking me with her—and I got a promotion, too!"

What about when you hear rumors that someone isn't doing his or her job, or that a colleague is being dishonest? Should you go to your boss then? That was certainly a dilemma Esther faced. But when Mordecai told her of Haman's evil plan, she didn't impulsively run to the king whining and pointing the finger at her adversary. In fact, had she done so, she likely would have been banished as queen—or worse, executed!

You definitely don't want to come across as a complainer or a tattletale, says Ken Lloyd, Ph.D., author of *Jerks at Work.* "Management hates that." Instead, present your boss with the problem— along with a solution. That way, you'll be viewed as someone who's constantly trying to improve things and help make your boss's job easier. The benefit? Even if he doesn't take your advice, he'll appreciate your take-charge attitude and will likely want to involve you in other problem-solving projects. That, in turn, should increase your visibility.

It's also perfectly okay to make remarks to others that you actually want your boss to hear. Helene, a senior accountant at a major publishing house, says, "A couple of months ago, I let it slip to a colleague that a headhunter had approached me to interview for a CFO position at a smaller publishing house. I wasn't all that interested in the position, because taking it would have required moving from New York to California. Still, sharing that news benefited me. I purposefully chose to tell a colleague who I knew had 'loose lips,' and soon my boss got wind of the fact that I was in demand. In no time, he called me into his office to tell me he didn't want to lose me. Then he offered me a host of incentives—a pay raise, greater responsibilities, and more vacation time—to stay."

You should never, however, tell a work friend anything that could have a negative impact on your job—or give your colleague power over you, says Jan Yager, Ph.D., author of *Friendshifts: The Power of Friendship and How It Shapes Our Lives*. "Men learn at an early age never to say or do anything that will derail their rise to the top, and women need to think in the same way if they want to climb the ladder."

The problem is, women come from a background of openness, or what Yager calls "coffee clutching." When we spill secrets to friends and coworkers, it's all in the name of bonding. But it's imperative that you develop a gut instinct for what may or may not be risky for others to know. "Just be savvy," says Yager. "Steer away from personal information and strong opinions as much as possible."

This means always dodging the "dirty dishing." Tempting as it may be to pass along juicy stories you hear—like who's having an affair, or who's secretly pregnant—spreading personal gossip can be harmful to others and poisonous to your professional reputation. That's because whomever you're spilling so-called secrets to, can't help but wonder what you could be saying about *them*.

Besides to establish credibility, you want to be viewed by higher-ups as someone who can be trusted—like Esther, who kept her promise to Mordecai to not divulge the fact that she was

Jewish to anyone in the kingdom. That she could keep a secret was a sign of character and strength and sets a sterling example for today's working women.

Another way to boost your credibility? Browder recommends going out of your way to squelch ugly rumors about others. "If you hear gossip about someone you know to be untrue, stand up and say so. By defending others from vicious smear tactics, you get a reputation for being high-minded, and word of your loyalty will likely leak back to your superiors," she says.

At the very least, she adds, remain neutral. When someone says, "Have you heard . . . ?" instead of adding to it, your response should be, "Oh really?" After all, an Indiana University study found that it's not the *opening* jab that sets the tone for a backstabbing conversation, but the comment made *after* the initial smear.

Using the "Zebra Rule" to Your Advantage

Ignore the grapevine, and you risk missing out on plum assignments and promotions because you're the last to get the news. Worse, you could miss signals that your company is in financial trouble and could be going belly up. In her book *If My Career's on the Fast Track, Where Do I Get a Road Map? Surviving and Thriving in the Real World of Work*, Anne Fisher calls this the "zebra rule." It's the zebra at the edge of the herd (think Haman!) that gets singled out by the lion, she explains.

Land on the right side of gossip—as Esther did—however, and you arm yourself with the latest map of the office so you can successfully navigate the issues. You can also align yourself with others who are "in the loop" and who will provide stability—and ideally—an upper hand to your place in the hierarchy. ♚

FIGHTING FOR WHAT YOU BELIEVE IN

*I*n Persia, it was customary for everyone to bow down not only
to the king but to his prime minister, Haman, as well. And
everyone in the kingdom complied—except Mordecai, as it vio-
lated his religious principles. So enraged was Haman with this in-
subordination, that he decided to kill Mordecai. And, upon learning
that Mordecai was Jewish, decided that all the Jews of Persia should
be put to death.

> When Haman saw that Mordecai would not kneel down
> or pay him honor, he was enraged. Yet having learned
> who Mordecai's people were, he scorned the idea of
> killing only Mordecai. Instead Haman looked for a way
> to destroy all Mordecai's people, the Jews, throughout
> the whole kingdom.
> —*Esther 3:5–6*

*The crafty Haman then took his plan to the king for approval.
Naturally, he didn't mention Mordecai by name. After all, doing so
might have foiled his evil plan, since Mordecai had saved the king's
life. Instead, Haman was vague about his target. And to ensure he
would get his way, he appealed to the king's need to replenish the treasury—which had recently been depleted by a disastrous war with
Greece—by offering him a bribe of ten thousand talents . . .*

Then Haman said to King Ahasuerus, "There is a certain people scattered and dispersed among the peoples in all the provinces of your kingdom; their laws are different from those of all other people, and they do not observe the king's laws. So it is not in the king's interest to let them remain. If it is pleasing to the king, let it be decreed that they be destroyed, and I will pay ten thousand talents of silver into the hands of those who carry on the king's business, to put into the king's treasuries.
—*Esther 3:9*

Ten thousand talents, biblical scholars tell us, is about 375 tons of silver—or roughly, the equivalent of up to 68 percent of the empire's annual revenue!

Despite that Haman had turned half-truths and exaggerations into outright lies, the king fell for it and agreed to Haman's plan. Delighted with this response, the callous Haman cast lots (purim) to decide which day this genocide should occur. He then convinced King Ahasuerus to give him his signet ring, which gave Haman the authority to issue an edict proclaiming the 13th day of the Hebrew month of Adar as the day all Persian Jews—men, women, and children—would be slain . . .

The royal secretaries were summoned. They wrote out in the script of each province and in the language of each people all Haman's orders to the king's satraps, the governors of the various provinces and the nobles of the various peoples. These were written in the name of the king himself and sealed with his own ring. Dispatches were sent by couriers to all the king's provinces with the order to destroy, kill and annihilate all the Jews—young and old, women and little children—on a single day, the thirteenth day of the twelfth month, the month of Adar, and to plunder their goods. A copy

of the text of the edict was to be issued as law in every
province and be made known to the people of every
nationality so they would be ready for that day.
—*Esther 3:12–14*

When Mordecai learned of Haman's plot, he went into mourn-
ing. True to Middle-Eastern tradition, he tore his clothes, put on
sackcloth, covered himself with ashes, and went out to the city
square, wailing loudly and bitterly. Esther's maids and eunuchs
spotted Mordecai and told Esther about his behavior. Confused
about the motives of his behavior, she sent him new clothes to put
on, but he refused them. So, Esther summoned Hathach, one of the
king's eunuchs assigned to attend her, and ordered him to find out
what was troubling Mordecai . . .

So Hathach went out to Mordecai in the open square of
the city in front of the king's gate. Mordecai told him
everything that had happened to him, including the
exact amount of money Haman had promised to pay
into the royal treasury for the destruction of the Jews.
He also gave him a copy of the text of the edict for their
annihilation, which had been published in Susa, to show
Esther and explain it to her, and he told him to urge her
to go into the king's presence to beg for mercy and plead
with him for her people.
—*Esther 4:6–8*

Hathach reported all of this to Esther, who was deeply distressed.
And despite Mordecai's pleas, she was also reluctant to approach the
king. She knew that going to him, unsummoned, could mean her
death. Moreover, she feared that she had lost favor in her husband's
eyes, as he had not called for her in a month. So she sent back word to
Mordecai explaining her position . . .

All the king's officials and the people of the royal provinces know that for any man or woman who approaches
the king in the inner court without being summoned
by the king has but one law: that he be put to death. The
only exception to this is for the king to extend the gold
scepter to him and spare his life. But thirty days have
passed since I was called to go to the king.
—*Esther 4:11*

*Mordecai was taken aback by Esther's reply and her reluctance
to go to the king, despite the risk she would be taking. He sent back
this answer . . .*

"Do not think that because you are in the king's house,
you alone of all the Jews will escape. For if you remain
silent at this time, relief and deliverance for the Jews will
arise from another place, but you and your father's
family will perish. And who knows but that you have
come to royal position for such a time as this?"
—*Esther 4:12–14*

*Ultimately, with the fate of her people hanging precariously in
the balance, Esther courageously accepted the mission of saving her
people, though doing so meant risking her life. And she sent this
message to Mordecai . . .*

"Go gather together all the Jews who are in Susa and fast
for me. Do not eat or drink for three days, night or day.
I and my maids will fast as you do. When this is done, I
will go to the king, even though it is against the law. And
if I perish, I perish."
—*Esther 4:16*

As queen, Esther could have pulled rank and easily ignored
Mordecai's plea to risk her life by appearing before the king
without an invitation. She could have also chosen to be selfish.

After all, heeding Mordecai's advice, Esther had not revealed to the king that she was Jewish. And as Carol M. Bechtel points out in *Interpretation: A Bible Commentary for Teaching and Preaching*, "If she does not reveal her Jewishness, then she could well escape by keeping silent. Or, perhaps there might be a less reckless plan for everyone concerned."

Instead, by deciding to go to the king when he had not called for her, Queen Esther took a huge risk, putting her position—not to mention her life—on the line. Think about it. Surely the fate of Vashti, her predecessor loomed large in her mind. And as Dianna Booher notes in *The Esther Effect*, "It had been thirty days since the king had invited her to his bedroom. Can you imagine the questions going through her mind? Did the king still find her appealing? Had someone more beautiful and entertaining replaced her as his favorite, and would he still love her if she spoke her mind?"

Indeed, this decision was a major turning point in Esther's life. Thus far, she had been little more than a young, sweet, and beautiful queen living the royal life of luxury—"hardly a person you would expect to shoulder her people's fate and engineer its salvation," says. Michael V. Fox, author of *Character and Ideology in the Book of Esther*.

What's more, from the onset, Esther's life had seemed entirely dependent upon and governed by males—from Mordecai, the cousin who raised her, and Hegai, the eunuch who oversaw her twelve months of beauty treatment, to her husband, the king whom she was expected to obey. Her opinions, her feelings, her thoughts were insignificant. Fox agrees. "She was putty," he says. "Not because of any personality flaw, but because of age and situation. Nothing had ever challenged her to be anything more."

Until now. Suddenly, by telling Mordecai to gather the Jews and fast for her, *she* was issuing commands—to Mordecai directly and to the community through Mordecai. As Fox notes, "she was now behaving as her cousin's equal and as a leader." Indeed, when it came to fighting for what she believed in, Esther was able to embrace the charge laid upon her. She was willing to take a huge risk—to lay her life on the line—by going to the king and blowing the whistle on Haman. And she decided to do all of this not because Mordecai had commanded her to do so, but because in her heart, and soul, and gut, she knew it was the right thing to do.

ESTHERS FOR TODAY

Recent headlines have been filled with stories of brave, modern-day Queen Esthers. Three who stand out as profiles of courage are Coleen Rowley, chief lawyer in the FBI's Minneapolis bureau; Sherron Watkins, a vice president at Enron, the bankrupt energy conglomerate; and Cynthia Cooper, vice president of finance at WorldCom. These courageous women blew the whistle on huge, powerful corporate machines—and none did it to advance her career. Instead, their missions were similar: to right some of the wrongs in their organizations. To them, sticking their necks out was a matter of principle, a question of ethics. And, like Esther, all three faced personal and professional peril.

"We Could Have Gotten Lucky"

As early as grade school, Coleen Rowley dreamed of working for the FBI, and fresh out of law school, she landed a job there as a special agent. She worked her way up the ladder to chief counsel in the Minneapolis field office, a major feat in this male-dominated bureaucracy. And by all accounts, she was pro-

fessional, highly disciplined, opinionated, principled, and extremely devoted to her job.

So devoted, in fact, that after 21 years on the job—and less
than three years from retirement—she made a bold move that
could have easily ended her illustrious career. Rowley fired off a
blistering thirteen-page letter to FBI director Robert Mueller
accusing the bureau of deliberately obstructing measures that
could have prevented the terrorist attacks of September 11.
Specifically, she charged that FBI headquarters in Washington
had stifled attempts of agents in her office to investigate Zacarias
Moussaoui, who was later charged with conspiracy in plotting
the terrorist attacks.

In mid-August, instructors at the Pan Am flight school near
Minneapolis/St. Paul had phoned local FBI agents to report that a
student with bad English had showed up asking for lessons on how
to fly a 747. Those agents forwarded this information to Rowley,
and she immediately instructed them to check out Moussaoui, who
was staying at a local hotel. A subsequent check of the suspect's im-
migration papers showed evidence of a possible visa violation, so
the agents arrested him on charges of overstaying his visa.

With Moussaoui in custody, Rowley and her staff launched
an investigation of the suspect's past. They quickly discovered
that the French police had placed Moussaoui on a "watch list" for
his ties with radical Islamic groups. Understandably, this red flag
prompted Rowley to request a warrant to examine Moussaoui's
laptop computer and other personal effects. Amazingly, FBI officials in Washington refused her request.

When the computer was finally examined after the 9/11 attacks, it was found to contain data about the cockpit layouts of
large commercial aircraft and telephone numbers, including one

for suicide pilot Mohamed Atta, one of Osama bin Laden's top henchmen.

Following the terrorist attacks, Rowley struggled with the decision to write her letter. By doing so, she realized she would be taking an enormous risk. Not to mention that she would be acting out of the chain of command. Clearly, it was not her place to directly confront the head of the FBI.

She wrote her letter at three o'clock one morning when she was unable to sleep. She then spent a week fine-tuning it, setting it aside for days, and agonizing over whether she should go through with it.

Ultimately, she flew to Washington to hand-deliver the letter to Mueller, two United States senators, and the staff of a congressional committee. In it, she described a "climate of fear" in the FBI. She also chastised her employer for obstructing the investigation of Moussaoui and called the FBI to task for misleading the public about who knew what and when.

"In the day or two following September 11th, you, Director Mueller, made the statement to the effect that if the FBI had only had advance warning of the attacks, we [meaning the FBI] may have been able to take some action to prevent the tragedy," she wrote to her boss. ". . . We could have gotten lucky."

"Although the last thing the FBI or the country needs now is a witch hunt," she added, the bureau must "come clean."

Rowley's letter was eventually made public, and she was called to appear before the Senate Judiciary Committee. While being interrogated, she was cool and articulate. Following her testimony, Republicans and Democrats alike praised her as a patriot, Americans hailed her as a hero. Major changes have since been implemented at the FBI, and while Rowley has no regrets for speaking out, she admits that doing so took a huge emotional toll on her.

"I am Incredibly Nervous That We Will Implode in a Wave of Accounting Scandals"

Sherron Watkins played a similar heroic role when she went public with her insights into the Enron scandal. In just eight years, this Midwestern mother of four had risen from accountant to vice president for corporate development at the Houston-based energy trading firm. But in August 2001, she too took a risk that could have sabotaged her career.

That same month, when the company's CEO abruptly resigned, Watkins discovered that the firm's numbers weren't adding up. Immediately—and anonymously—she wrote a memo to new CEO Kenneth Lay, warning him that his predecessor's sudden departure had tongues wagging.

"I am incredibly nervous that we will implode in a wave of accounting scandals," Watkins said in her memo. "I have heard from one managerial-level employee from the principal investments group say, 'I know it would be devastating to all of us, but I wish we would get caught. We're such a crooked company.'"

Indeed, turns out that in an effort to support its inflated stock price, Enron had hidden billions in debts and operating losses.

Lay's reaction to the anonymous memo? He assured Enron employees that the company was on sure footing. Simultaneously, behind the scenes he was exercising stock options—buying low, selling high, and netting about $1.5 million over a two-day period.

Meanwhile, Watkins sought advice from a colleague at Arthur Andersen, Enron's accounting firm. She then decided to acknowledge sending the anonymous memo and requested a meeting with Lay. She arrived at that late-August meeting with a six-page letter detailing her concerns, which Lay promised to have the company's lawyers investigate.

By the end of September, the company's stock was plunging. Nevertheless, Lay assured Enron employees that "our financial liquidity has never been stronger." In mid-October, however, Enron disclosed a $618 million loss in the third quarter and a $1.2 billion reduction in shareholder equity. What's more, some employees were barred from selling Enron stock in their 401(k) plans—supposedly because the company was switching plan administrators.

In reaction to the company's staggering losses, the SEC quickly launched an inquiry, and the finger pointing began. Fortunately, Watkins had a paper trail proving what really went wrong.

In February, Watkins was subpoenaed to testify before a House Energy and Commerce subcommittee, where she called her company "the poster child of corporate abuse." Indeed, the fallout of Enron's collapse was huge. Scores of employees found themselves out of a job. Worse, as a result of the company's devastating stock plummet, billions were lost in retirement funds.

She Took Down a Telecommunications Giant by Doing the Right Thing

She's been described as "totally honest" and "full of integrity" by friends, neighbors, and former teachers. So it's no surprise that Cynthia Cooper didn't hesitate to blow the whistle on telecommunications giant WorldCom.

Growing up in Clinton, Mississippi, Cooper always had a knack for numbers. But she never imagined that a Fortune 500 company like WorldCom would build its headquarters in her hometown—or that she would someday be their vice president of finance.

Actually, that was a title she had long aspired to. Cooper had first joined WorldCom (then known as Long Distance Discount

Service—LDDS) in the early 1990s as a consultant in the finance department. But she left for a short time to join paging company Skytel before returning to LDDS in the mid-1990s to run its internal audit department. A former executive at the company told the *Wall Street Journal* that Cooper was motivated and dedicated, telling LDDS management at the time, "I want to be a vice president some day."

In fact, she climbed the ranks at WorldCom to vice president of finance, and it was in that position—during a routine audit—that Cooper noticed some questionable transferring of funds. She immediately discussed these disturbing findings with her boss, then CFO Scott Sullivan. He tried to explain to Cooper why costs that had previously been expensed were suddenly being capitalized. Then he asked her to delay her audit for a few months, but she refused.

Turns out, what Cooper had uncovered was a scheme to disguise nearly $4 billion in expenses from the investing public, a ploy that allowed WorldCom to post profits when it was actually losing millions!

Cooper, who felt she had no choice but to alert the company's board to this phony accounting scheme, did so with a heavy heart. WorldCom quickly began to unravel and eventually declared bankruptcy—the largest in U.S. history.

"YOU'LL NEVER WORK IN THIS INDUSTRY AGAIN!"

Rowley, Watkins, and Cooper publicly exposed wrongdoing in three of the highest-stakes cases in the country. What motivated these women to endanger their careers and personal status for the greater good? And how did they summon the courage to take such extraordinary risks?

Granted, there are laws in place designed to protect whistle-blowers from retaliation. But according to Fred Alford, author of *Whistleblowers: Broken Lives and Organizational Power*, an estimated 90 percent of whistleblowers face repercussions. It is not uncommon for them to be blacklisted, harassed, socially ostracized, demoted, or even fired.

For example, Sherron Watkins was ridiculed by her bosses in Houston. And, like Esther—who told Mordecai, "If I perish, I perish"—Coleen Rowley also feared reprisal. "Due to the frankness with which I have expressed myself . . . I hope my continued employment with the FBI is not somehow placed in jeopardy," she wrote in her memo.

Whistleblowers often pay a hefty emotional and mental price for donning that badge of courage as well. Lifetime friends may turn against them. Colleagues may treat them as outcasts—even when their actions are in coworkers' best interests.

So, why take such risks? For most, it's a matter of integrity, ethics, and morals. "Whistleblowers tend to have a strong sense of right and wrong," says attorney William L. Bransford, of Shaw, Bransford, Veilleux and Roth. "Their strength of conviction and this sense of right and wrong propels them forward." Whistle-blowers also tend to be tough, gutsy, and totally unselfish. "They're typically unwilling to back down in the face of threats and reprisals," Bransford adds. "They want a resolution that not only protects their jobs and their livelihoods, but also protects everyone who has been endangered or exposed to unfair treatment."

WHAT'S GENDER GOT TO DO WITH IT?

Is it significant that the prominent heroes to emerge from the three great organizational scandals of recent years were women? Actually, there *is* evidence that suggests gender does play a role.

One prominent theory is that of the insider-outsider. "Women aren't part of the 'good ol' boy' system," says Kris Kolesnik, executive director of the National Whistleblower Center in Washington, D.C. "What's important to them is doing their job, not protecting their buddies."

Adds Rutgers University anthropologist Helen Fisher, Ph.D., author of *The First Sex: The Natural Talents of Women and How They Are Changing the World*, "Women aren't as sensitive as men to status in the workplace. And when you're not as committed to the hierarchy, you can see the ramifications a little better."

In fact, Fisher believes that, thanks to social conditioning, women may be natural whistleblowers—because of the way they think and how they learned to play as children. "As young boys, men jockey for position in the playground and learn early on to give and take orders," she explains. "If boys don't like the rules, they leave the game. Girls, on the other hand, play in leaderless groups, not hierarchies, and choose games with far fewer rules, which change if someone gets upset. Subsequently, as adults, women aren't likely to play by the rules if they don't think the rules are right."

According to Alford, another factor that makes women statistically more likely to speak out and fight for what they believe in is that they typically have one foot firmly planted in another world: the family. This, he says, connects them to a different way of thinking. "In fact, when they bring that model of ethics into an organization, it must put a lot of women through hell."

While researching his book, Alford found that male whistleblowers talked in terms of "tortured loyalists," because they

ROYAL ADVICE

I work as an executive assistant for a high-ranking city government official. I have evidence that my boss has been taking bribes from construction companies in exchange for information on how low to bid on major local government projects. I'm tempted to blow the whistle on my boss, not only because what he's doing is unethical, but if he gets caught, people could assume I was guilty by association. As a single mother with three children to support, however, I can't afford to lose my job. Any advice?

Of course, you should stand up for what you believe is right and make a decision of conscience. However, you are right to recognize that blowing the whistle *can* be risky, and by telling the truth, there *will* be consequences. You could lose your job, be ostracized by your colleagues and superiors, pounded by the press, and face a lengthy legal battle.

Before taking any action, review your options. Is there a reasonable way to work within the system and avoid going public with your concerns? You may also want to consider making an accusation anonymously—although these are more difficult to investigate, and nothing may come of it.

To prepare for the fallout, consult an attorney who can explain your rights and help you navigate the legal system. Make sure you have sufficient information to back up your claims. Keep a log you can refer back to for specific details, witnesses, dates, and times to prove your point.

For more information, we recommend you check out *The Whistleblower's Survival Guide* at www.whistleblower.org.

had been raised as team players. Women, on the other hand, talked about the dichotomy between the home, where they care for the family, and the office, where everything seems overly to do with profit.

University of California professor Judith Rosener believes that "women tend to see things in a much bigger context than men do." In her e-book *Ways Women Lead*, she notes that women also tend to see the implications of the decisions—such as who will be hurt—in contrast to men, who tend to think about whether they will make money or get caught. "Not that men are more crooked," she adds. "They just don't think about implications in the same way."

Nancy Evans, cofounder and editor-in-chief of iVillage, agrees. Speaking at the Trailblazer Roundup of Women in Corporate America, a conference organized by the Business Women's Network, headquartered in Washington, D.C., she remarked, "Women tend to be straight talkers and sensible problem-solvers, and they raise the flag if something doesn't add up."

RISKY BUSINESS: WHY WOMEN ARE, BY NATURE, A CAUTIOUS LOT

Many women, as these inspiring stories prove, are willing to risk everything when ethical issues are involved. Yet, when it comes to taking risks for professional advancement or personal gain, women, as a rule, hesitate to take risks. Instead, most prefer to play it safe.

For example, when Hagberg Associates, a Foster City, California, consulting firm surveyed more than 300 senior managers and executives about personality characteristics and management styles, they found that while women scored significantly higher overall than men as managers and leaders, they were averse to risk-taking.

What gives? Researchers like Paul Slovic, Ph.D., a professor of psychology at the University of Oregon, chalk it up to social conditioning. In his studies, Slovic examined the risk-taking behavior of children between the ages of six and sixteen and found no difference among the youngest boys and girls. But by the age of nine, boys took more risks than girls did. "This leads me to believe that women make take fewer risks because our culture doesn't encourage them to," he says.

Jeanette Scollard, author of *Risk to Win: A Woman's Guide to Success*, agrees. "The very word scares women. When I give a lecture, I sometimes ask what risk means to my audience. Invariably, the men answer 'success' or 'opportunity,' but the women say 'fear' or 'failure.'" Indeed, the word "risk"—which comes from the Italian word *risco*—means "unknown origin." And unfortunately, women frequently fear the unknown.

"But every woman in business today needs to take risks, because it means you're moving, growing, changing," adds Scollard. "And things do change—your company, the way it does business, the marketplace. If you don't take chances, if you bury your head, you'll be obsolete and out the door. Today, it's inactivity that's the real risk."

HOW TAKING RISKS CAN BOOST YOUR STATUS

"Success in today's business economy demands nonstop innovation," believe Richard Farson and Ralph Keyes, coauthors of *Whoever Makes the Most Mistakes Wins: The Paradox of Innovation*. "But fancy buzzwords, facile lip service, and simplistic formulas are not the answer. Only an entirely new mindset—a new attitude toward success and failure—can transform managers' thinking. And the key to this new attitude lies in taking risks. The best way to fall behind in a shifting economy is to rely on what's worked in the past."

In other words, marching in place no longer cuts it. Success today requires you to be a change agent. You gotta shake things up a bit and make a few waves. And, like Queen Esther, you must be willing to take a leap of faith. Only then can you discover your true destiny.

Diane Creel's story is an excellent case in point. When named president and CEO of Earth Tech in Long Beach, California, she became the world's first female CEO of a publicly traded engineering firm. What's more, she landed her position with three strikes against her. "I was a woman, I was not an engineer, and I came from marketing," she explains.

What got Creel noticed—and promoted—was the fact that she was a champion risk-taker: a leveraged buyout of the company founder, five acquisitions in 27 months, a push into several new businesses, and overseeing Earth Tech's sale to a larger company.

The secret to her success? Embracing change. "It's a constant in any business," she says. "And I try to view it not as a threat but as an opportunity and a challenge."

Irene Esteves, CFO of the Boston money-management firm Putnam Investments, Inc., agrees. "If you want a high-profile job, you have to go where the bullets are—where there's a bigger chance of failing." Esteves did tours at packaged-good conglomerate SE Johnson & Son, Inc. and Miller Brewing Company before taking on the CFO role at Putnam. "The position at Putnam was too attractive to turn down, but I charged into an industry I didn't know," she admits.

"Taking the difficult path is what gets women noticed. People assume men naturally want challenges; women often have to seek them out," adds Diane Price Baker, who is credited with taking Macy's in and out of bankruptcy and helping close the sale of the company to Federated. She also joined the *New York Times* at a precarious time. "They were actively working against themselves. They had to recast how they looked at themselves both internally and externally," she says. Under her reign, the company's stock soared from $21 to $73 a share.

How to Tell a Good Risk from a Bad One

When Queen Esther approached the king, unsummoned, she could have been put to death. When Rowley, Watkins, and Cooper blew the whistle on the FBI, Enron, and WorldCom respectively, they could have been put through the same hell Anita Hill was when she accused Supreme Court nominee Clarence Thomas of sexual harassment, or Linda Tripp was when she exposed Monica Lewinsky's affair with President Clinton. "If [corporate executives] had had more time, they would have done what every organization does against a whistleblower: mounted a case and done the old rumor and innuendo routine on [these women]," acknowledges Kris Kolesnik, executive director of the National Whistleblower Center in Washington.

Likely, all these women—Esther included—pondered worst-case scenario outcomes, but ultimately decided theirs were risks worth taking. And obviously, all felt that sticking their necks out was the right thing to do.

So, following your heart is one key to determining a good risk from a bad one—particularly when moral issues are involved. In other instances, the answer isn't always so crystal clear. But the majority of women who have gotten ahead by taking risks agree that in most cases, to take a risk—or not to—boils down to following your gut.

That's what Katharine Graham, the late chairwoman of the *Washington Post* Company did when she decided to publish the Pentagon Papers. Prior to 1963, Graham was a self-described "doormat wife." Then her husband, who suffered from manic depression, committed suicide. Rather than sell the newspaper her father had rescued from bankruptcy in 1933—and which her husband had run since her father's death—she decided to take it over herself.

Never mind that she had no business training and was ill-equipped to run a corporation. In time, she emerged as the first lady of American journalism.

When Graham first took charge at the *Post*, however, it was privately owned with little national standing. Her advisors recommended that the paper issue a stock with diluted voting control, and while she wasn't crazy about the idea, she agreed to do it. Then, on the eve of the IPO, the *Post* was handed the Pentagon Papers.

Her lawyers cautioned her not to publish them, arguing that such a move might jeopardize the *Post's* new standing as a public company. Moreover, the Nixon White House exerted tremendous pressure on the *Post* not to publish the papers. Graham took the risk anyway because she felt it was the right thing to do. The story *had* to be told, she believed—even if telling it meant standing up to the Nixon administration. Ultimately, publishing the Pentagon

Papers kicked off the investigation of the Nixon administration. The *Post* won a Pulitzer for the Watergate story, profits soared, and Graham eventually emerged as one of the most powerful women in America.

FREEING YOURSELF FROM FEAR OF FAILURE

Surveys show that the number one reason women avoid taking risks is—you guessed it—fear of failure. Fortunately, there are ways to overcome this fear.

One option: being passionate about your work. "When you believe in what you're doing, embracing change and taking risks are much easier," says Jane Hamilton, who is CEO of Prudential Institutional and one of nine executive vice presidents at the company's parent, Prudential Insurance Company of America. "Passion allows you to push forward, to take the leap to what you know is right in your heart. If you don't have that passion, when it comes time to make the tough decisions, you'll be afraid to make them. You won't do what you know has to be done because you don't feel it in your heart. You won't be willing to take the risk and say, 'This is what has to be done; this is the right thing to do.'"

Another option: Gamble just once—even if the cards seem stacked against you, advises Shirley Clarke Franklin, the first female mayor of Atlanta, Georgia. "Then do everything possible to make your risk pay off. When others see you acting daring, their respect for you goes through the roof."

Franklin should know. She put her consulting company on hold, shelled out $80,000 of her own money, and spent two years campaigning.

Better still, embrace your fear head-on, by reminding your-self again and again, "Nothing ventured, nothing gained." And take comfort in the fact that you are following in the footsteps of some super-successful women.

"While at AT&T, one assignment had me scared for two years," admits Carly Fiorina, now chairman and CEO at Hewlett Packard. "I was managing a government contract, and we were suing a customer. I was terrified of failing at that one. It was the formative experience of my career because I conquered my fear."

Visible risk-taking like this, she adds, "lets people know what you're doing and what you're capable of. I found out—and others did, too—that I could learn a whole bunch of new things in a hurry. I also learned that you don't have to be an expert to be ef-fective, you just need to learn and to get help from the right folks."

FOCUS ON THE FOREST, NOT THE TREES

When contemplating a risk, always look at the "big picture," as Esther did. She took a calculated risk. Or, as Booher puts it, "She knew her facts. She assessed the situation. She saw the significance of what she was about to attempt. She counted her cost."

According to the 300-plus senior managers and executives polled by Hagberg Associates, however, women are far less likely to take risks unless they've covered all the bases. Sound familiar? This approach is fine, but you don't have to be a perfectionist.

"Women can easily get mired in the details in an attempt to make sure everything is handled correctly," the study found. In essence, "women's penchant for doing their homework may lead to better decisions, but it can also backfire by making them seem rigid."

Prudential's Hamilton concurs. "It's important to learn to make decisions quickly and in a timely way. This means knowing how much information you really need to make a decision without overanalyzing it."

So, go ahead—take at least a tiny risk you have a strong gut feeling about, and don't agonize over it—even for a second. Women in positions of power do this all the time and say it's the quickest way to get comfortable taking risks. As the great Golda Meir, former prime minister of Israel, once said, "I can honestly say that I was never affected by the question of the success of an undertaking. If I felt it was the right thing to do, I was for it, regardless of the possible outcome."

Another modern-day Queen Esther who took a leap of faith and kept her focus on the big picture is Deborah Lipstadt. This well-respected Dorot Professor of Modern Jewish and Holocaust Studies at Emory University made international headlines when she was sued for libel by British historian David Irving. In her book *Denying the Holocaust: The Growing Assault on Truth and Memory*, Lipstadt named Irving as one of a group of anti-Semites who had devoted their careers to denying that the Holocaust had taken place or who argued that historians had vastly overstated the extent of its devastation. He subsequently sued Lipstadt for libel in London, where *defendants* bear the burden of proof (versus the United States, where plaintiffs must prove statements made about them are false).

Lipstadt believes Irving chose her because he thought she wouldn't fight back. "I'm a woman, a Jewish woman, an American Jewish woman. He thought I would crumple, and fold, and give up," she told *The Jerusalem Post*.

He thought wrong. Like Esther, Lipstadt chose to challenge evil. Never mind that it took a twenty-man team of lawyers, paralegals, and secretaries to fight this injustice. Never mind that standing up for what she believed in cost Lipstadt five tortured years of her life. "It was my duty, my responsibility," she says.

In the end, the judge agreed with Lipstadt's evaluation of Irving as a Hitler apologist, Holocaust denier, and liar. In fact, the judge's 355-page verdict, she says, "proved far stronger than anything I wrote about Irving." Irving was also forced to pick up the $3 million tab for Lipstadt's defense.

"This battle came and found me," Lipstadt adds. "Had I not fought, he would have won by default. He then would have been able to say that he was correct. I decided to fight it with all my strength and all my might. Not fighting was never an option, to let evil go unchallenged." ⚜

MAPPING OUT YOUR PLAN OF ATTACK

A fter fasting for several days, Queen Esther donned her finest robes. She was trembling as she dressed. She knew that she was taking an enormous risk by approaching the king. She also knew that if her husband was not happy to see her, she could die.

Slowly, she made her way to the inner court of the palace, in front of the king's hall. King Ahasuerus was sitting on his royal throne in the hall facing the entrance. And fortunately, he was pleased to see his bride . . .

> And it happened when the king saw Esther the queen standing in the court, she obtained favor in his sight, and the king extended to Esther the golden scepter which was in his hand. So Esther came near and touched the top of the scepter. Then the king said, "What is troubling you, Queen Esther? And what is your request? Even to half the kingdom, it will be given you."
> —*Esther 5:2–3*

The king's response brought Esther a huge sense of relief. Still, she chose not to cut to the chase. Instead of bringing up the fact that Haman was plotting to kill all the Jews, Esther took the indirect and

seemingly passive approach—by inviting him and his counselor
Haman to a banquet . . .

> And Esther said, "If it pleases the king, may the king and
> Haman come this day to the banquet that I have prepared
> for him."
> —*Esther 5:4*

King Ahasuerus was delighted with Esther's invitation and sent
for Haman at once.

Later, at the banquet, as they were drinking wine, the king—his
curiosity piqued—again asked Esther what was on her mind . . .

> "Now what is your petition? It will be given you. And
> what is your request? Even up to half the kingdom, it will
> be granted."
> —*Esther 5:6*

Biblical scholars tell us that "up to half the kingdom" is a polite
way of saying, "Even if your request is a large one, I will do it." This
was the moment Esther was waiting for—the perfect opportunity to
point the finger at Haman. But she didn't tell her husband what she
wanted, Instead, Esther asked only for a second banquet with the king
and Haman the following day and promised to reveal her wish then
and there . . .

> Esther replied, "My petition and my request is this: If the
> king regards me with favor and if it pleases the king to
> grant my petition and fulfill my request, let the King and
> Haman come tomorrow to the banquet I will prepare for
> them. Then I will answer the king's questions."
> —*Esther 5:7–8*

At this point in her story, it's hard not to notice Esther's transformation from a powerless queen to a brave and courageous

leader-in-the-making. "The fate of the Jews is now as much hers as Mordecai's," notes Carol M. Bechtel, in *Interpretation: A Bible Commentary for Teaching and Preaching.* "Finally, she shows the resolution and self-possession of a true queen." This is even reflected in Esther's language as she is in control and begins to use commands. When she tells Mordecai to gather the Jews and fast for her, for example, and when she proclaims, "If I perish, I perish!" this "reads like a battle plan, and she is clearly the general," Bechtel adds.

Indeed, Esther has taken charge and clearly has a well-designed plan in mind to save her people. In fact, many biblical scholars agree that this queen was a brilliant strategist.

How so? For starters, she could have easily sent a messenger with a written request for an audience with the king. But she didn't—and with good reason. "Then she would have had to state the purpose of her visit, and that would have tipped the king off," explains Dianna Booher in *The Esther Effect.*

She could have barged into the throne room and insisted on speaking to the king immediately. Instead, she donned her royal robes and lingered just outside the door, hoping to catch her husband's eye. This purposeful hesitation probably worked to Esther's advantage, Bechtel believes, in that "it gave Ahasuerus the illusion that it was his idea to invite her in." Very clever, indeed.

Fortunately, the king extended his golden scepter to Esther, welcoming her into his chambers. Obviously, he was in a good mood, so why did Esther put off telling the king what she wanted? Likely, she was buying some time. Clearly, it would be to her advantage for the king to forget her sin of uninvited entry. Quite possibly, she also wanted to delay making her request until such time as the king, under the influence of wine, was in a good mood and more willing to comply with her wishes.

Why invite Haman to dinner? Wouldn't Esther be more likely to get her husband to agree to her request at an intimate dinner for two? Probably not. Suppose the king had listened to her request, then agreed to get back to her after giving Haman a chance to tell his side of the story. That would have been disastrous for sure. As Bechtel says, "There would have been no way of guaranteeing her presence at such a meeting, and thus no opportunity to press her advantage. This way, she can catch Haman off guard, giving him no time to concoct an excuse or to wriggle out of it later when it's 'just between us guys.'"

Of course, another reason Esther invited Haman to the banquet may have been for her own benefit. Surely, doing so gave her a secret sense of self-satisfaction, for by seeming to honor her arch enemy, she was, in reality, setting him up for his downfall!

Finally, what's up with the two banquets? Maybe Esther got cold feet at the first dinner. Keep in mind that she faced a delicate dilemma: accusing Haman without incriminating the king, who had, after all, sealed Haman's decree of death for the Jews with the king's full knowledge and approval. Or maybe she merely had a gut feeling at the first banquet that the moment just wasn't right.

Women today can glean valuable lessons from Esther's strategic ways. She knew that success doesn't just happen; you have to make it happen. You need a game plan and strategies to help you get what you want—and where you want to be. In essence, your battle for upward mobility must be carefully orchestrated.

So, what techniques can you employ in modern times to ensure you achieve your desired outcomes? In plotting out your battle, we suggest taking advantage of these military maneuvers:

DECIDING YOUR MISSION

Esther's mission was crystal clear, and to get what you want out of life, you need to make your own personal mission statement, says Laurie Beth Jones, author of *Jesus, CEO: Using Ancient Wisdom for Visionary Leadership*. "Having a clearly articulated mission statement gives you a template of purpose that can be used to initiate, evaluate, and refine all your activities. A mission statement forces you to reexamine who you are . . . and what you are really about."

Indeed, everyone—from a corporate CEO to a small business owner to a PTA president—needs a personal mission statement, believes military hero and Secretary of State Colin Powell, who, like Esther, rose to power from humble beginnings. "In the military, to 'close with the enemy' means to identify your opponent, then organize your resources to fight," writes Oren Harari, Ph.D., author of *The Leadership Secrets of Colin Powell*. "In more general terms, it means identifying goals, then taking steps to achieve them. Once you have a sense of direction, you can select strategies that will help you reach your goals. Without this guiding vision, you are wasting your time."

EARNING YOUR STRIPES BY EXERCISING PATIENCE

In many Bibles, there is a noticeable block of white space between Chapters Four and Five in the ancient Book of Esther. Charles R. Swindoll, author of *Esther: A Woman of Strength and Dignity* calls this a "grand pause—a space of suspense when we don't know what is happening, because nothing is recorded for us to read."

We believe this royal pause symbolizes that patience can pay off royally. Surely, when Esther first approached the king—and certainly at the first banquet—she was eager to point the finger at her nemesis, Haman, and put an end to her ordeal. Instead, she purposefully put off naming her request to the king because stalling was part of her strategically laid-out plan. Moreover, Esther's rise to power was slow and deliberate—and she is far from alone.

Every year, *Fortune* magazine releases a list of the Fifty Most Powerful Women in Business, and in 2001, a new kind of leader emerged: strong and resolute—but definitely not in a hurry. "We see the emergence of women who came to power slowly," the editors wrote. "We're not talking about women who had the patience to suffer indignities or who sat passively in an out-of-the-way corner. Rather, they stayed with a company, steadily building influence there, and rose to power through determination and insider knowledge. . . . Through a combination of deep knowledge of the corporation, personal humility, and will, they created enduring greatness."

Amy B. McIntosh's story is a perfect example, In her rise to CEO of Zagat Survey, LLC, New York, providers of international restaurant and nightlife guides, McIntosh says she did some purposeful job-hopping and exercised patience. "I managed my career to get a wide variety of experiences," she told the *Wall Street Journal.* "For instance, while I worked at American Express as the vice president of marketing, I deliberately moved to Phoenix so that I could get operations experience at the company's call center. Later, I went to Nynex to learn about technology. Making these kinds of decisions gave me the ability to jump into new situations and get the learning curve down quickly." McIntosh's atypical route to success—and the broad range of knowledge and know-how that came about as a result—also likely helped to groom her for a CEO position.

VISUALIZING YOUR SUCCESS

Chances are, Esther also used the "royal pause" to mentally rehearse her conversation with the king—and to visualize herself succeeding at her mission. You can do the same to get the results you want and deserve.

In fact, neuroscientists have found compelling new evidence that proves mental practice can actually increase real-world performance. In his book *Mind Sculpture*, author Ian Robertson, Ph.D., describes a recent study in which people who mentally practiced a five-finger piano exercise (their fingers never actually touched any keys) were compared with those who physically practiced. Results? Both groups showed improvements in accuracy. What's more, both showed an increase in size in the areas of the brain that control finger movement.

This means that merely visualizing positive results in our minds actually strengthens our neural circuits—those millions of neurons firing in concert that are involved in successful performance. Thus, if you can generate positive pictures in your mind, this rosy outlook literally gets you positive results—first in your brain, and then in your performance!

In her climb up the ladder to become the first female president of a Hollywood studio, Dawn Steel, former president of Columbia Pictures, often used this technique to boost her confidence. "One of my great tricks was that before I walked into a room, I would picture the people in it applauding me—you know, for whatever—I had done something that made them welcome me into the room. And so when I got to the room, I had made myself more comfortable by that image that I kept in my head. And it always worked. I would take a deep breath and play a part."

NEVER RULING OUT "SNEAK" ATTACKS

A sneak attack on Haman was certainly key to Esther's master plan. Had she forewarned him about the accusations she was prepared to throw his way, he might have come up with an excuse to wiggle his way out of wrongdoing—or pointed the finger at someone else.

Modern-day Queen Esther Deborah Lipstadt understood the wisdom of the sneak attack as well. When Holocaust denier David Irving took her to trial for libel, her defense team also masterminded a sneak attack. The tactic that ultimately spelled Irving's demise: submitting questions about evidence during pre-trial interrogations for him to answer—questions that they knew he couldn't answer truthfully on the stand. He either had to lie, or admit to the court that he had lied earlier. It was a brilliant move that left Irving very little "wiggle" room.

KNOWING WHEN TO TAKE COMMAND

When Esther was first crowned queen, Mordecai advised her not to divulge her ethnic origins to anyone. But all that changed once Mordecai learned of Haman's plot to have all the Jews in Persia slain. "Speak!" he advised Esther. "Plead with the king. Stop this plot against our people."

Esther did speak up, but many women are reluctant to do so. The problem? In her book *Talking from 9 to 5*, Deborah Tannen points out how early socialization of girls—to be "seen and not heard" or not to speak out in class—can have serious repercussions later in business.

Indeed, women frequently wait until the "right moment" at meetings to present ideas. Or worse, we never speak up at all. Yet, as Betty Spence, president of the National Association of Female Executives, points out, "What seems like good manners at a meeting keeps women's knowledge unacknowledged."

Paula E. Groves, a Harvard Business School graduate who worked on Wall Street and in Hollywood before hooking up with another woman to start their own venture capital firm in Boston, Axxon Capital, concurs. "At a venture capital firm where I used to work, I was the only woman among eleven men," she recalls. "It was very easy for me to clam up and not say much. One time the company was considering financing a company that I was against, but I didn't speak up. The deal went forward and later their client declared bankruptcy. That experience taught me the importance of rising above insecurity and making my contribution."

Even former Secretary of State Madeline Albright admits that during White House meetings early in her career, "I would think of something and not say it. Then some man would say what I had been thinking, and it would be applauded."

Successful women have learned, however, that getting ahead requires speaking up—as Esther did when it came down to fighting for her life and her people.

The same holds true for pulling rank—another issue that tends to intimidate women, who much prefer a "let's work together" approach.

Liz Dolan agrees. She is a former vice president of global marketing at Nike who now cohosts—with her four sisters—Satellite Sisters, a popular public-radio talk show and is the co-author of *Satellite Sisters' Uncommon Senses*. "At Nike, I once had a difference of opinion about the company's strategy for a particular project with an employee who headed that project," she says. "And at the end of our tenth conversation, he finally said,

ROYAL ADVICE

I was recently appointed to sit on the finance committee at work. At meetings, I've come up with several good ideas, but I rarely get credit for them. Why does this happen, and what can I do about it?

What often happens at meetings is that one person's idea quickly becomes the "group's" idea. Or, frequently with women, someone else (typically male) takes credit for their ideas. To avoid this—and get the credit you deserve—always arrive at a meeting with your idea summarized in outline form on paper, and put your name at the top of the page. Make enough copies to distribute to everyone at the meeting, and lay them face down in front of you. Pitch the idea, and if it bombs, leave the papers where they are. If, however, your idea goes over well, pass them out by saying, "I've got the key points in writing. Let's build on this."

'Well, Liz, I guess you and I just disagree.' That was the moment of truth for me as the boss because I thought, 'Okay, we just disagree. Does that mean I fold? Or do I just say my vote counts more than yours?'"

Ultimately, Dolan did tell her subordinate, "You're right, we disagree, so here's the way we're going to do it. It was one of the hardest things that I ever did," she admits. "As women, we are raised to be the peacemakers. Our instinct is to find common ground, but sometimes it just doesn't work."

Working around the Rules

Esther faced a real dilemma. She had to approach the king, un-summoned, which was against Persian laws. Nevertheless, to get what she wanted, she had no choice but to break, or at least bend, the rules—and only by doing so, was she ultimately successful.

Unfortunately, in modern bureaucracies, men tend to be more skilled at working around the rules and navigating red tape if clearing such obstacles will increase their visibility or status. "I learned a lot about this issue when an Associated Press business reporter informed me that nine out of ten men say yes to interviews, while nine out of ten women say no," writes Betty Spence, president of the National Association of Female Executives in one of her columns for *Executive Female*. "What's more, when companies tell employees not to talk to the media, women comply, but men defy it. In fact, men go to PR departments to become spokesmen for the company. They request—and receive—tailored media campaigns and training. But women rarely do this."

Devising a Battle Plan

Breaking the rules by approaching the king without an invitation required Esther to come up with a no-fail plan. After all, her life was at stake! And somehow, she managed to figure out a way for her husband to extend to her the golden scepter and welcome her into his royal chambers.

In your own career, when it comes to pitching ideas or trying to win someone over to your point of view, you, too, must figure out the best way to approach people—from bosses and colleagues to clients and boards of directors. To do this, Harry Mills, author of *Artful Persuasion: How to Command Attention, Change Minds, and Influence People*, recommends using a personality-typing approach, which entails pinpointing your "audience's" type and approaching them accordingly. "This will allow you to speak in the language and context most favored by the other person," he explains. And you're far more likely to be successful.

For example, when approaching a person who's known to be abrupt and short tempered, your best bet is to gain some credibility and neutralize their views. On the other hand, if you're dealing with someone who's apathetic, your goal is to energize and motivate him or her. "Some people are persuaded by the power of detail," Mills adds, "while others are mostly moved by the big picture."

Even humor can go a long way when attempting to win others over to your side. For example, when Carol Lopucki took over as State Director of the Michigan Small Business Development Center, she became the first woman ever to hold that position. "Prior leadership had been very rank and file, top down in style, and there I was walking into meetings following eighteen years of this style of doing business," she recalls. "In the early days, I can't tell you how many high-level meetings I walked into where folks were ready to slice me up before I even started to speak."

Lopucki came up with two strategies that worked well for her. "Once I stood outside the door waving a white flag before entering the room. This quieted the group down, made people smile, plus gave me the chance to get the first words out and set the tone I wanted," she reports.

"Nowadays, when I know I'm walking into a fire, I begin the meeting by saying, 'Okay, you have exactly ten minutes (pointing to my watch as if to start the timer) to dump everything on me

ROYAL ADVICE

Having worked in middle management for nearly five years, I'm long overdue for a promotion and anxious to move up the ranks. My performance evaluations have always been above average, but when vacancies become available, I'm typically passed over. In fact, in almost every instance, I've lost out to someone with less seniority—usually a male candidate. What could I be doing wrong?

You need more feedback. What are your strengths and weaknesses—not as you see them, but as viewed by your superiors? What expectations do your boss and your boss's boss have of you, and how can you best fulfill these expectations? Where do you fit in the big picture? These are questions you should be asking during your performance evaluations, but don't wait. Ask for feedback continuously—after completion of every project, following a presentation, after leading a meeting. Women assume that promotions will be handled fairly, so they don't ask questions. Men ask what they need to do to move up.

you think is relevant from the past. At nine minutes, I will give you a warning that time's almost up. I will listen attentively and give no comment.' Then, I ask, 'Can we move forward . . . without moving backward?'"

This has been a great strategy, she adds. "I get people in both camps: some laugh and say, 'Okay, you got me; let's just move forward.' Others take me up on my offer and use every ounce of the ten minutes they've been promised. But I've never had anyone go backwards!"

BEING READY WITH A BACKUP PLAN

What if King Ahasuerus had not been pleased to see Esther? Worse, what if he had denied her request to "come this day to the banquet" she had prepared for him? Surely, Esther wouldn't have given up. Her request was far too important to accept no for an answer. In fact, it's likely that Esther had a backup strategy in place to achieve her goals.

Winning your career battles requires following in Esther's footsteps by devising strategies to get what you want and not taking no for an answer in critical matters. Yet, as Gail Evans points out in her book *Play Like a Man, Win Like a Woman*, "Men learn at an early age that 'no' has a range of meanings: no, maybe, or later. But the female definition of the word 'no' is often absolutely not, how could you even ask?"

Brianne Leary had a secure career as entertainment co-anchor of *Good Day New York*, and—like the rest of us—remembers exactly where she was on September 11, 2001. "I was organizing a man-on-the-street shoot to ask New Yorkers what they thought about Mayor Giuliani's divorce," she writes in an article for *O, The Oprah Magazine*. When the first plane hit the World Trade Center, Leary had a hunch that Osama bin Laden was behind the attack. Years earlier, she had worked in Afghanistan as a freelancer for *TV Guide* and had plenty of sources there.

As the story unfolded, Leary's hunch proved to be correct. She jumped on the Internet and made contact with two of her connections. General Abdul Rahim Wardak, former chief of staff of the Afghan military, promised her an exclusive interview.

And Mujahideen commander Abdul Haq pledged to give her any assistance she needed.

Immediately, she relayed all of this information to the news director at her station. "I told him about my previous experience inside Afghanistan and offered to help with this developing story," she says. "He politely took my e-mail printouts and said, 'We'll see.'"

While awaiting her boss's decision, Leary hoped—at the very least—to change the focus of her man-on-the-street interviews to report heartbreaking encounters with victims' families. But that idea was also turned down, when her executive producer reminded her that she had been hired "to make people laugh."

When days passed with no word from her boss, Leary decided to go over his head and meet with the general manager of Fox. She expressed her concern of being stuck with lightweight assignments and mentioned her connections in Afghanistan. "He claimed to understand my desire to go to Afghanistan, but turned me down, citing money as the main reason," she says. Yet, soon after that, Fox hired Geraldo Rivera to go.

Not one to give up so easily, Leary contacted a friend who put her in touch with Eason Jordan, head of international news gathering for CNN. After a phone call and face-to-face interview with him, she was told that many of CNN's more experienced journalists were eager to go to Afghanistan. "But he didn't say no," she says.

Two weeks went by, however, with no word from Jordan. "I was doing stories on how to rake fall leaves and make the perfect martini. Then, on November 13—as Kabul was falling—I was reporting on Girl Scout cookie-selling season." At that moment, Leary realized she needed to be doing something more substantial with her life. So she booked a flight to Pakistan with plans to leave two days later. "I needed time to pack, get organized, walk out of my Fox contract and convince Jordan to give me the assignment," she says. The next morning, she called Jordan at the crack of dawn and talked nonstop for five minutes in an effort to convince him to say yes. Finally, he told Leary, "Okay, go."

Leary spent five weeks in Afghanistan filing "day-in-the-life" stories for CNN. "I felt I'd make the most difference by bringing the faces of the Afghan people into the homes of Americans. Now that I am back home, each day I say a prayer never to forget those five weeks, and to remember how I got there."

INCREASING YOUR VISIBILITY

Queen Esther requested not one, but two banquets with King Ahasuerus and Haman. Why? Putting in more face time with the king before revealing her request was likely part of her master plan.

Smart strategy, says Ronna Lichtenberg, author of *Work Would Be Great if It Weren't for the People: Ronna and Her Evil Twin's Guide to Making Office Politics Work for You*, who believes that one of the best ways to increase your visibility at work is to set your face time by your boss's clock. "Years ago, I realized that my boss's boss stayed late on Friday afternoons, waiting out the rush hour. Everyone else bailed out early, but I stayed. The big boss and I ended up having regular Friday chats. Over time, I got to share with him ideas he wouldn't have had time to listen to during regular business hours. After a dozen Fridays, I got the resources I needed to put some of those ideas in place—including responsibility for another department."

Human resources consultant Virginia Means shares a similar story. "When I was just coming up in the business world, I met a very successful CEO of the hospital system for which I was employed. After he had observed some of my work, he asked me to take on several projects while the company opened some additional hospitals in the community. During this time, he really took me under his wing. For example, while working on the projects, I would sometimes get frustrated with situations—most often because people seemed to be dragging their feet on decisions, and things were not moving fast enough for me. And I would often go to him for counsel."

These counseling sessions most often occurred "before the roosters woke," Means says, "as we were both morning people. In fact, that seemed to be the time that he was most open to dialog and giving advice. He was too busy with conference calls and meetings in the heat of the day and too exhausted after six o'clock."

Another way to increase your visibility? Schmooze in the office. "Women are such dedicated, hard-working implementers that they work nose-to-the-grindstone without crossing the boundaries," says Jean Otte, founder and president of Women Unlimited, Inc. "This means they miss out on learning about other parts of the business or having those in other parts of the business know about their skills. As a result, women sometimes don't understand the big picture the way that men do, because men take the time to make those strategic alliances."

Many women also mistakenly believe that if they work hard, they'll be rewarded, Otte adds. "But they're finding out that it's not what you know; it's who you know. If you're brilliant and no one knows, what good does it do?"

As a case in point, Otte shares the story of a senior-level vice president who was left without a job after a recent merger of two major corporations—despite the fact that she was one of the hardest-working executives at the company. The reason for her loss? "This woman stayed within her unit to such an extent that people from the rest of the company really didn't know her," says Otte. "So, she was passed over a job in the merged organization." The lesson here? Schmooze, or you could lose.

Researchers at the University of Cincinnati and Pennsylvania State University agree. In their studies, they found that office workers who take the time to venture out of their department for a chat are likely to receive better evaluations from their bosses. That's because these "cross-pollinators" are able to bring fresh ideas to their departments and know how to act on them.

BUILDING ALLIANCES

Esther had at her beck and call an entire delegation of maids and eunuchs. In fact, it was through these palace personnel that she learned of Vashti's downfall—and how to avoid her predecessor's mistakes. She also gleaned from them priceless information about her new husband—what pleased him, what didn't, and how he made decisions. Moreover, it was through this support staff that Esther communicated back and forth with Mordecai—and discovered that the fate of her people hung in the balance.

Today we call this process networking, and studies show that it can catapult your career.

Indeed, at least 75 percent of jobs are landed through networking, according to Atlanta career coach Jennifer B. Kahnweiler, president of About YOU, Inc. "And that even includes jobs advertised in the newspaper and through search firms," she says.

What's more, among women who have participated in Women Unlimited programs (this firm offers networking opportunities to women from companies across the country), networking can have an incredibly positive impact on your career. All agreed that through networking, they not only broadened their circle of contacts, they also gained the confidence to ask for promotions and raises, the courage to pursue other opportunities within their companies—plus they improved weaknesses and developed strengths.

The good news, according to Helen Fisher, Ph.D., author of *The First Sex: The Natural Talents of Women and How They Are Changing the World*, "Women don't have to learn how to network—they're born with the ability. On a playground, it's the little girls who form groups and work to build harmony within their tight circles."

Despite this natural affinity to click and connect with others, however, networking is not a high priority for many women because it requires time and energy—two precious commodities among a majority of working women today.

Nevertheless, in today's ever-changing business economy, networking is a necessity in your quest for success. "It's critical throughout your career to gather information and to let people know of your interests so they'll have their radar up for you," says Peter Vogt, prescient of Career Planning Resources, a career counseling firm in Eden Prairie, Minnesota.

But what if you don't have time to put on the power suit and go out to shake hands and pass out business cards? Kahnweiler offers one solution. "You want to be strategic about how you network. It used to be you just networked all over the place. Let's meet this person, let's meet that person. But our time is more valuable now. You want to be smarter about how you network."

Another option for women busy juggling work and family is to log onto their computers to network. The Internet is an invaluable tool for connecting with other professionals, reaching potential clients, and learning more about your industry. Many online sites have chat rooms with scheduled meetings—or you can network on your own using message boards and forums. If you're on America Online, go to the "Your Business" section to browse chat listings and find a group you'd like to join. For other service providers, try doing searches for a topic that is of interest to you and include "chat," "message board," or "forum" as a keyword when you search. (Examples: "business chat," "marketing message board," "real estate forum.")

Better yet, create your own network online. That's what Janet Hanson did when she left Wall Street investment firm Goldman Sachs to launch her own money management firm, Milestone Capital Management, in Yonkers, New York.

Her site, www.85broads.com (the name refers to Goldman's Manhattan address, 85 Broad Street), is exclusively for current and former employees of Goldman Sachs and provides a place for female financiers to chat and network. "It's like a clubhouse," says Janet. Members can browse categories such as "Show Me the Money," a place to hunt for venture capital; "R & R," where members swap travel tips; and "Top Broads," which profiles Goldman alumnae who have started their own companies.

Hanson says she has received thousands of requests to join her site from women not affiliated with Goldman Sachs. "There is a huge demand and need for these networks," she says. "Whether women are working or taking time off, they need to be able to connect with other successful women who have gone before them."

For this reason, Hanson and her husband have since launched two other sites: Broads and Wall (www.broadsandwall.com) is for women in the financial services industry; Broads and Main (www.broadsandmain.com) is for women who work in Fortune 1000 corporations. "These Web sites are not networks in themselves," she says, "but they provide the software tools for women to develop their own at no cost." A third site for women entrepreneurs is on the drawing board.

Yet another popular solution to the time-crunch challenge entails mixing business with pleasure. For example, many women have formed small groups called "Girl Gangs," that get together regularly in person, by phone, and even via e-mail. Betsy Beaumon, an electrical engineer who worked for Lam Research and Cisco Systems before starting an Internet company, selling it, and then joining another start-up as vice president, is part of a girl gang. The group formed several years ago, she says. when Beaumon decided to hook up with five other women who seemed to be at every trade show she attended.

"Our group communicates almost daily by e-mail," she reports. "We even get together and slam down a goodly number of cosmopolitans when the opportunity arises."

The purpose of their girl gang is to help each other navigate the ever-turbulent waters of high technology. "We exchange ideas on office space and phone systems, as well as share advice on cultural issues within startups and technology companies," Beaumon says. "It's an interesting dynamic when the group is together, and it's helpful to have someone you can bounce ideas off of and explain how things work. With my current job at a startup, it was great to have friends who knew how to negotiate stock options and salaries for a high-level position."

For many women, networking is all about cultivating relationships, celebrating personal and professional successes, and sharing information in a safe, noncompetitive environment.

But strategic networking is also about making contacts, finding new leads, striking deals, and fitting in. And the good news is, there's certainly no rule that says you can't meet all of these goals simultaneously.

Shelly Lazarus, CEO of the advertising giant Ogilvy and Mather Worldwide, for example, certainly doesn't let the fact that she's a busy wife and mother prevent her from networking. In fact, she often uses it to her advantage. Over dinner at four-star French restaurants with potential clients, for example, Lazarus is known for warmly asking questions about their families—as well as sharing stories about her husband and three children. Once, she even engineered a blockbuster deal—in which IBM switched all its accounts worldwide from an assortment of smaller agencies to Ogilvy and Mather—at the beauty shop!

"Abby Kohnstamm [IBM's vice president of corporate marketing] and I had been having coffee and talking for years," says Lazarus. "We'd chat about this and that." Then, one day while the two were getting a manicure together, Kohnstamm decided to give Ogilvy the $500 million account. ♛

6

COMMUNICATING
WITH THE CLOUT
OF A QUEEN

*H*aman left the palace bursting with pride and ego and wasted no time assembling his wife and friends for a bragging session. He boasted about his vast wealth, his many sons, and all the ways the king had honored and elevated him above all the other nobles and officials . . .

> "And that's not all," Haman added. "I'm the only person Queen Esther invited to accompany the king to the banquet she gave. And she has invited me along with the king tomorrow. But all this gives me no satisfaction as long as I see that Jew Mordecai sitting at the king's gate."
> —*Esther 5:12–13*

Hearing this, his wife and pals had a suggestion, which delighted Haman . . .

> "Have a gallows built, seventy-five feet high, and ask the king in the morning to have Mordecai hanged on it. Then go with the king to the dinner and be happy."
> —*Esther 5:14*

Meanwhile, Esther was pacing the palace, filled with apprehension. She knew she had to tread carefully with her plan to outwit

Haman. After all, accusing the king's closest advisor without bringing the king's wrath down on herself was a delicate and dangerous task. So, she was relieved when, at the second banquet, the king repeated his original offer . . .

> "Queen Esther, what is your petition? It will be given
> you. What is your request? Even up to half the kingdom,
> it will be granted."
> —*Esther 7:2*

Boldly, she made her move—choosing her words carefully for maximum impact . . .

> "If I have found favor with you, O king, and if it pleases
> your majesty, grant me my life—this is my petition. And
> spare my people—this is my request. For I and my people
> have been sold for destruction and slaughter and annihi-
> lation. If we had merely been sold as male and female
> slaves, I would have kept quiet, because no such distress
> would justify disturbing the king."
> —*Esther 7:3–4*

The king was furious that the life of his beloved wife and her people had been threatened and demanded to know . . .

> "Who is he? Where is he, who would dare presume in his
> heart to do such a thing?"
> —*Esther 7:5*

Esther turned and pointed toward you-know-who, and replied . . .

> "The adversary and enemy is this vile Haman!"
> —*Esther 7:6*

Considering that she lived in biblical times when women were expected to be passive and submissive, Esther had surprisingly powerful communication skills and used these to capture the king's attention. How did she do it? By understanding her audience . . . by doing her homework . . . by carefully selecting her words . . . by stating her case directly . . . and by asking for what she wanted.

But it wasn't always so. As her story has developed, so has Esther's sense of responsibility and leadership—and this is clearly reflected in the power of her language.

Think back, for example, to when Mordecai first instructed Esther to go to the king and plead for the life of the Jews. She didn't give him an immediate answer—most likely because she was concerned about her safety. But after much soul searching, she resolved to do her duty, and immediately a change came over her. "She *commands* Mordecai—in the imperative, with no polite circumlocutions—to assemble the Jews in Susa for a public fast," notes Michael V. Fox, author of *Character and Ideology in the Book of Esther*.

In fact, this is a major turning point in Esther's story. Henceforth, she is the one—not Mordecai—calling the shots. "She now behaves as Mordecai's equal and as a leader of the community," Fox adds.

In her book *Interpretation: A Bible Commentary for Teaching and Preaching*, Carol M. Bechtel also praises Esther as a powerful communicator. "Esther is patient in implementing her plan of attack. She is brilliant in her analysis of her enemy's methods. And finally, she is every bit his equal in her power to persuade. Esther's character is so strong by now, that we almost begin to feel sorry for Haman. But not quite."

Women today need to employ the same powerful communication skills that Esther did to get what they want. Whether handling negotiations or confrontations, attempting to impress others, or persuading someone to your point of view, success requires communicating with the clout of a queen—and that involves:

AVOIDING SPEECH PATTERNS THAT CAN SABOTAGE YOUR CREDIBILITY

When Esther told Mordecai to gather all the Jews in Susa and fast for her, she didn't hedge or pepper her speech with qualifiers—*I suppose, I guess,* or *I'm not 100 percent sure, but . . .* —as that would have made her sound weak, uncertain, and uncommitted. Nor did she end her request with a tag question—*This could work, Mordecai, don't you agree?* Women typically use tags to avoid confrontation, to try to please everyone, or to get others to buy into their agenda. But using tags can make you seem unsure of yourself.

When Esther approached the king, she exuded confidence. She didn't diminish herself by saying, "You may not like this, but . . ." In fact, she completely avoided using disclaimers—those introductory expressions that excuse, explain, or request understanding. You know them only too well: *I'm not 100 percent sure about this but . . . I may be wrong about this but . . .* or *This may be a stupid question but . . . .*

There is no faster way to diminish your credibility than using disclaimers. Not only does it dramatically decrease your level of influence, it invites listeners to disagree or not take you seriously. After all, if *you* think it's a stupid question, inevitably, they will, too.

Nor did Esther's speech contain fillers—*um, ah, like, well, uh, er, y'know, kinda,* and *sorta.* Researchers say women use these in much higher proportions than men do, particularly when we address men—and usually out of fear of coming on too strong.

Fillers, however, signal uncertainty and lack of preparation. They also open the door to interruption.

Instead, Esther was firm and decisive, and as a result, she commanded respect and got what she wanted.

As a powerful communicator, Esther also made a point of gathering her thoughts before she spoke. At the second banquet, for example, when the king asked Esther what was bothering her (*What is your request?*), she wasn't vague or tentative, and she didn't ramble—as women tend to do when they are nervous and trying to sell themselves or their ideas. Nor did she overwhelm him with details. Instead, she gave him the executive summary.

Nonstop chatter can also make you seem unfocused and egocentric, says Sharon Voros, author of *The Road to CEO: The World's Leading Executive Recruiters Identify the Traits You Need to Make It to the Top.* "For example, when an interviewer asks, 'What have you accomplished?' you don't need to review your entire career—just offer a few highlights."

Fox agrees and notes that in response to the question, *Who is he? Where is he, who would dare presume in his heart to do such a thing?* King Ahasuerus only wanted to know who the guilty party was. "His concern is not for the endangered people, and not even primarily for Esther's safety, but for the royal honor."

Indeed, can you imagine Esther going to the king and kvetching about what a jerk Haman was? Such a ploy surely would have had her banished from the kingdom—just like Vashti!

USING BODY LANGUAGE THAT SAYS "I MEAN BUSINESS!"

When Esther first approached the king, she arrayed herself in "*malkut*—regal apparel, not merely attractive clothes," notes Fox, who suspects she wanted to remind her husband of the royal dignity he had conferred upon her when he crowned her queen. "For an affront to her royalty would be an insult to his," he explains.

She also *stood* before the king, rather than kneeling at his feet. "Her stance in itself reminds the king of her royal status. This was her subtle way of reminding him that she was approaching him as Queen of Persia."

Marsha Londe, vice president of Promotional Products for Atlanta-based Summit Marketing, uses powerful body language as well when she's getting ready for battle. "When I'm in the 'I'm-the-boss' mode, I deliberately change my body language and my voice. I hold myself more erect, face the person squarely, and lose the smile in my voice. Shouting and loud ranting are unacceptable. Instead, I consciously lower my level and speak more deliberately so that the other person knows I mean business."

TRUSTING YOUR INTUITION

Before taking out Haman, Esther had two other chances to bring him down—when she first approached the king and he held out his scepter, and then at the first banquet. Instead, she kept quiet. Why? "This is a wise woman who understands the value of timing," says Charles R. Swindoll, author of *Esther: A Woman of Strength and Dignity*. "The time wasn't right. Esther had a sensitive ear, a wise heart. She sensed something wasn't quite right. So, she didn't push it. She knew when to act—and she knew when to wait."

Do you know when to roll with the hunches and trust your sixth sense? Scientists have actually uncovered evidence that women's intuition really does exist. One psychological study conducted at Harvard University, for example, found that those who are more subordinate in conversations—generally

ROYAL ADVICE

My boss recently called me into his office and criticized my management style. He said he was concerned about the high turnover rate among my staff and that morale in my department was low. Some of what he said is true; still, his stinging words devastated me. In fact, when he proceeded to give me some advice, I hardly heard a word of it because I was too busy biting my lip in an effort to remain composed. How can I learn to handle criticism without falling apart?

Constructive criticism is a tool that can sharpen and refine your skills, as well as encourage professional growth. Nevertheless, it still feels like punishment and women are especially vulnerable because we tend to take it personally.

Next time this happens, take a couple of deep breaths and try these strategies to keep your composure.

First, repeat the criticism—"So you're saying that I may be doing something to alienate my staff." This not only helps you clarify what you've heard, it also gives you time to calm down. Next, decide if you agree or disagree with the criticism (you have every right to disagree, but do it tactfully). Finally, if you agree, say so, then add what you're going to do about it—"I'll check into the situation, determine what's happening, and see that your concerns are addressed."

If the criticism has caught you by surprise and you're afraid of overreacting or becoming an emotional basket case, give yourself an opportunity to calm down before you respond. To do this, simply say, "I'd like some time to think about what you said. Let's talk again tomorrow morning."

women—were found to be more sensitive and intuitive toward whoever was perceived to be the leader, thus increasing their interpersonal sensitivity.

"In my workshops, I have observed that part of women—that deep, intuitive, ancient feminine knowledge and wisdom—waking up," says Eliana Harvey, who runs Wise Women workshops in Dorset, England. "In fact, once women start to tap into this sixth sense, their decisions in life are usually right-on," she believes. "Things start to go better for them, and extraordinary coincidences and connections start to happen."

Ten Pearls of Wisdom author Eleanor Jacobs, for example, was rejected not once, but twice for what she calls "the breakthrough job of my career." But something kept telling her, "This is your job," she recalls. "So I kept focused on it. I stayed in touch. I networked. Some days I would walk over to that office building and just stand in the doorway, the vibes were that strong."

When the position came open the second time, it went to another candidate. Jacobs was told she'd been the second choice. "I couldn't believe it," she recalls. "I couldn't let go." Within days, the new hire had a change of heart, and the position was hers. "Now, even when there are limiting factors, even when there are doubts, I've learned to trust that inner voice, that higher consciousness," she says.

Jacobs admits that she might never have won this coveted job but for her fierce determination in pursuing it—and that's the point. "Intuition, that inner voice whispering its wisdom, is one thing, but it is useless in our lives without our good faith effort to actually create through our actions the most positive outcome we sense possible," Jacobs says. "If we truly believe in our ability to bring about our highest good, we can actually send vibes out into the universe that can set events in motion. Our beliefs, as well as our actions, have creative power."

MEETING YOUR "ENEMIES" HEAD-ON

Most women aren't comfortable with confrontation or conflict, but sometimes the only way to get someone's attention or to address a sticky situation is to be bold. Esther, for example, chose to clash with Haman face to face by inviting him to the banquet where she planned to expose him to the king. Good move, notes Bechtel. "She realizes that she must certainly prevent him from parleying with the king (and others) behind her back. She must get events moving so quickly that the momentum will sweep the wishy-washy monarch into action."

PLAYING TO YOUR AUDIENCE

Esther understood her husband's vulnerabilities and even took advantage of them. For example, at the second banquet, when she made her plea to the king, it was masterfully constructed. By first underscoring the danger to her own life, she appealed to King Ahasuerus's affection for her. Next, she grabbed her husband's attention by suggesting that he was about to lose the person dearest to him and most intimate with him. Then, only when this approach succeeded, did she expand it to include her entire threatened race.

You can employ this same strategy in your negotiations—by finding a way to address the answer to "what's in it for me?" in all your pitches. Another strategy for playing to your audience is to subtly "mirror" the other person's movements and to respond by using many of the words and phrases they use. Studies show this goes a long way at establishing rapport and strengthening connections. Esther certainly used this strategy with the king. For example, when he asked, "What is your petition . . . what is your request?" she answered by mirroring his exact words: "My petition is . . . and my request is . . ."

ALWAYS DOING YOUR HOMEWORK

Another reason Esther delayed voicing her request to the king was that she might not have trusted him—or his generous offer—to grant whatever she wished. And her feelings were certainly justified. As Fox points out, "In the past, the king has shown himself both mercurial and malleable." Indeed, remember how her predecessor Vashti was treated? When the former queen defied the king's orders, he turned to his advisors for counsel on how to handle the situation, and Vashti was banished and replaced as queen.

So, while Esther knew her husband to be impulsive, she was also keenly aware of his tendency to seek counsel from his advisors before making major decisions. Such hesitancy could be disastrous in this case, notes Fox, as Haman and others would surely work on the king and probably succeed in making him retract his offer. Esther realizes by playing her cards right, however, that she may be able to steer her husband's impulsiveness in the right direction.

When Esther made her plea to the king—*For I and my people have been sold for destruction and slaughter and annihilation*—she proved, once again, that she had done her research. She knew the exact terms of Haman's edict and even used the exact language—*destruction, slaughter, and annihilation*—in her appeal. Moreover, it's obvious that she had practiced her speech and knew exactly what she was going to say.

When pitching ideas at work, you can also increase your odds of getting what you want by doing your homework, says

ROYAL ADVICE

I just took a job as a buyer for a large department store. One of my primary responsibilities is to negotiate with vendors to get the best prices. While I have limited experience at negotiating, I do know the importance of doing my homework and playing to my audience. But what about settings for negotiations? Aren't there definite advantages to meeting on my turf?

Not necessarily. Conventional wisdom says you should always do this, because it places you in a position of control. But meeting on your opponent's turf offers many more advantages, and you get a lot of clues about people you're negotiating with by checking out their surroundings and seeing how they treat their staff. Also, if and when things get hot, you're in more control. You can walk away from the negotiating table, something that can't easily be done if you're negotiating in your office.

Rita Craig, chairwoman of the Florida Commission on Human Relations. She advises having a "pre-sell" meeting to help you gain confidence in your idea and assurance that it will be well received. "Women aren't as good as men in having conversations before meetings about what projects they want approval for and why. Do this, however, and you'll score big!"

Craig says she once watched a female executive do this perfectly. "Prior to her presentation, she had checked with everyone attending the meeting. She commented that she had spoken and listened to every individual and was open to hearing whatever they had failed to mention right then and there. She said, 'I want to make sure you feel comfortable about this decision.' At that point, she gave everyone a handout with all the options, pros and cons, and her ultimate recommendation. It sailed right through because it was obvious she had done her homework and taken care of their concerns. And the fact that she had a document for them to look at reinforced her position."

KNOWING HOW TO TALK SO PEOPLE WILL LISTEN

Getting the king to listen to her was key to Esther's success. But as every woman knows, this can be challenging. It's a problem even the most powerful executive women face.

For example, when Sandra Day O'Connor became the first woman to be named to the Supreme Court, she confessed to a reporter that getting her male colleagues to listen was her biggest challenge. "I taught myself early on to speak very slowly—enunciating every word—when I wanted someone's undivided attention," she said.

Why do women feel so ignored? Deborah Tannen, author of *Talking from 9 to 5*, chalks most of this up to social conditioning. Having been raised to be nice and polite, women tend to smile and wait their turn to present an idea, she explains. "Many women also expect listening to be reciprocal: 'I listen to you now; you listen to me later. Then they become frustrated when they do the listening now and now and now—and later never comes."

The best way around this is to be one of the first to speak. "Get an idea out on the table quickly, and you become a presence up front," says Tannen. "Moreover, when you speak up, hit the central point of your idea first—and hit it hard," she adds. Studies show that women have a tendency to add too many details and not get to the point quickly enough—a style that causes men to tune out.

Following this advice served Esther well. By the time Esther pointed the finger at Haman, she had the king on the edge of his seat. "A less carefully crafted statement might have begun with the story of how Haman had taken offense at Mordecai and sought the destruction of the Jews as an outgrowth of his vendetta, and so forth," acknowledges Bechtel. And while such an approach would have made sense in terms of sequence, it would not have been nearly as effective. By cutting to the chase instead, she makes sure the king understands that her life has been threatened. Her words both shock and inform."

SETTING THE STAGE SO YOU CAN TAKE CONTROL

When Esther suggested to the king that he and Haman join her for dinner, he was quick to agree and could hardly hide his excitement. Fox notes that Esther's move to host this banquet poses "an interesting question of who comes to whom, a theme introduced when Vashti refused to come to the king and was banished. Now it is the king who comes to Esther's banquet."

Isn't she clever? Esther knew that hosting a banquet would move her pending conversations with the king to her turf; she would be in charge. She also knew that her husband loved to eat and drink and felt certain that such a setting would make him more compliant.

Indeed, at the second banquet, by the time the king once

again asks Esther what is bothering her, he is merry and mellow with wine. "Esther has him right where she wants him," Bechtel remarks.

PICKING YOUR BATTLES

"Esther did not exercise power for the sake of power. She didn't concern the king needlessly on a whim or with a whimper," says Booher. Moreover, when she made her plea to the king, she appealed to his pride by inferring that he was far too important to bother with a mere sale of innocent people (including herself) into slavery. Rather, it's their destruction, slaughter, and annihilation that has brought her to petition in her own—and their—behalf.

Picking your battles is a lesson Virginia Means, former managing director of human resources for a Fortune 500 company, says she learned early in her career. "My mentor used to tell me, 'Before you take things to the next level and create discussion around an issue, or complain that things are not moving at the pace you think is necessary, remember—you only have so many arrows in your quiver.' In other words, fall on your sword only when absolutely necessary."

"You see, I tended to identify issues and wanted to remove the obstacles pronto," she continues. "The problem is, that is not necessarily the way the business world works. There are people, process, culture, history, and impact (PPCHI) to consider. The other very valuable piece of advice my mentor gave me was, 'Time is on your side.' My take away from that was to avoid bringing up issues or problems too soon because many of them are likely to take care of themselves. However, you have to be aware of PPCHI in order to know when to reach for the arrow. And sometimes you need to let the little ones go so that you have the arrows and control to bring home the big game."

RECOGNIZING THAT A LITTLE BIT OF CHUTZPAH GOES A LONG WAY

Have you heard the one about the little old Jewish lady who gets onto a crowded bus and stands in front of a seated young girl? Holding her hand to her chest, she says to the girl, "If you knew what I have, you would give me your seat."

The girl gets up and gives her the seat to the old lady. It is hot. The girl then takes out a fan and starts fanning herself. The woman looks up and says, "If you knew what I have, you would give me that fan." The girl gives her the fan, too.

Fifteen minutes later, the woman gets up and says to the bus driver, "Stop, I want to get off here." The bus driver tells her he has to drop her at the next corner, not in the middle of the block. With her hand across her chest, she tells the driver, 'If you knew what I have, you would let me off the bus right here." The bus driver pulls over and opens the door to let her out. As she's walking out of the bus, he asks, "Madam, what is it you have?"

The old woman looks at him and nonchalantly replies, "Chutzpah."

We define chutzpah not as rudeness or disrespect for others but as the ability and courage to make gutsy and clever moves— even play the drama queen if need be—for the purpose of attracting attention to get what you need and deserve. Esther had chutzpah when she finally told the king what was bothering her—that her death and the death of her people has been ordered. But she deliberately did not use Haman's name. Her intention? To build suspense and let the king work himself in to a rage and decide the villain's fate before he knew the villain's identity. How clever is that?

And when her husband demanded to know who the culprit was, she dramatically pointed the finger at Haman.

Used in the right way, chutzpah can catapult you to success. The problem is, most women are reluctant to be daring and bold. Not Dorrit Bern, CEO of Charming Shoppes, Inc., a Fortune 1000 company that sells retail women's apparel. Earlier in her career, this marketing expert was hired by Sears to boost sales. One of the ideas she developed and implemented was "The Softer Side of Sears" campaign, which revolutionized the marketing strategy at Sears to focus on products that appeal to women.

Her marketing plan not only changed the product lines available at Sears, but also the positioning of various products within any Sears store. For example, jewelry counters displaced lawn mowers, and cosmetics displaced paint.

Bern joined Sears with the blessing and mandate of the corporation's Chairman/CEO, and she enjoyed his support for her new directions. "Needless to say, this did not sit well with several of the 'old guard' men who were resistant to the new, softer approach, which muscled out their product lines and their floor space," she recalls.

In fact, one of the senior executives in charge of hardware products refused to make floor space available for Bern's product lines—despite a company directive for him to do so. "Rather than bringing this up with the CEO, or holding this executive accountable under those directives, I challenged him to a game of golf to determine who would get the floor space," she says. "The loser would relinquish the floor space to the winner."

Little did Bern's nemesis know, she had played professional golf before starting her career in marketing. And, as you might have guessed, she handily won the match. What's more, not only did the male senior executive end up relinquishing the space, he also ended up relinquishing his job!

Bern went on to make history in the annals of American marketing for her talent in identifying the value of the women's market and setting the standard in providing services and products to meet the needs of this market. She is now one of only a handful of women ever to serve as a Fortune 1000 CEO. ♛

7

DEALING WITH LIFE'S HAMANS

*A*rrogant. Ruthless. Manipulative. Not surprisingly, Haman's name, translated from the Hebrew, means "wrath." A vicious anti-Semite with an evil temperament, Haman was outraged when Mordecai refused to bow down to him. So, he tricked King Ahasuerus into signing a decree to kill all of Persia's Jews by telling the king half-truths. "There is a certain people . . . they do not obey the king's laws," he told the king, then convinced his boss that it was not in the king's best interest to tolerate these people.

When the king agreed, Haman callously cast lots to decide the timing of the event he believed would seal the fate of Persian Jews forever.

But Haman's fate was about to change. At the second banquet, when Queen Esther pointed the finger at him for ordering the destruction of the Jews, the king was outraged—and his prime minister terrified . . .

> The king got up in a rage, left his wine and went out into the palace garden. But Haman, realizing that the king had already decided his fate, stayed behind to beg Queen Esther for his life.
> —*Esther 7:7*

In a flash, matters went from bad to worse for Haman. As the king went out to the garden to take a breather, the villainous Haman tried to beseech Esther to show mercy. As he approached the couch she was sitting on, he clumsily fell upon her—just as the king was returning. The king assumed Haman was trying to make a move on Esther in his absence, which infuriated him even more.

> Just as the king returned from the palace garden to the banquet hall, Haman was falling on the couch where Esther was reclining. "What, would you even ravish the queen right here in the house with me at home?" the king exclaimed.
> —*Esther 7:8*

Haman was humiliated—and speechless. As the king pondered Haman's fate, Harbona, a eunuch—and one of the little people Esther had befriended—piped up with this suggestion . . .

> "A gallows seventy-five feet high stands by Haman's house. He had it made for Mordecai, who spoke up to help the king." The king said, "Hang him on it!" So they hanged Haman on the gallows he had prepared for Mordecai. Then the king's fury subsided.
> —*Esther 7:9–10*

Haman is long gone, but cunning and conniving folks like him continue to exist today. Beastly bosses . . . jealous subordinates . . . competitive coworkers. But here's how to outsmart modern-day "villains"—and triumph in spite of them.

WHEN BAD BOSSES HAPPEN TO GOOD PEOPLE

Bad bosses make for great Dilbert cartoons, but they're no laughing matter when you're the victim. And, chances are, you've worked for at least one big-time jerk in your career.

Join the club! In a recent survey conducted by Delta Road, a corporate coaching firm in Denver, Colorado, an amazing 81 percent of employees described their supervisors as lousy managers.

What a shame, since according to a Gallup poll of more than one million employees, how long workers stay at companies—and how productive they are—is determined by their relationship with their immediate supervisor.

Bad bosses come in many packages—the most common being the Control Freaks, the Cutthroats, and the Tyrants. And all pose a considerable problem and cost to companies and workers alike.

"Bad bosses are the number one reason people chuck their jobs and look for new ones," says Michael Useem, author of *Leading Up: How to Lead Your Boss So You Both Win*. Which means that working for a jerk can certainly hinder your advancement. How so? By preventing you from reaching your full potential, for starters. And/or by causing you to job hop more than you'd like, which consequently forces you to explain to potential new employers what went wrong with a boss from hell.

Bad bosses can also seriously damage a company's bottom line. Studies show that in terms of recruiting and training new hires alone, replacing just one employee can cost six months or more of that worker's salary. Not to mention how corporate creeps affect absenteeism or employees' morale and productivity levels—as well as workers' psyches in terms of self-esteem and stress levels.

"If a school teacher is abusing students, we get rid of him or her," says Gregory P. Smith, founder and president of Chart Your Course International, a Conyers, Georgia, training and consulting firm. "Same with a doctor who's killing patients. Why is it that management is the only field in which we tolerate bad behavior, even when it costs companies lots of money? It's because we have the attitude that people are expendable."

Bad bosses can be particularly harmful to women, since when problems arise, we tend to blame ourselves and wonder, "What am *I* doing wrong?." Or, as confrontation-avoiders, we might bury ouselves in our work, pretending that our boss doesn't irritate the hell out of us.

The good news is that most bad bosses aren't that way on purpose. "It's just very, very hard to be a good boss, and many people are thrown into the role with little or no training," believes Suzy Wetlaufer, former editor of the *Harvard Business Review*. Many are also under a lot of pressure from their own bosses and clueless as to how annoying or overbearing they can be. "Sometimes just simply making your boss aware of problems can lead to significant improvement in self-knowledge, flexibility, and understanding of others," says Richard Boyatzis, chair of the organizational behavior department at Cleveland's Case Western Reserve University.

So, the trick to preventing a bad boss from sabotaging your career lies in taking control of the situation—and here's how to do just that.

CONTROLLING CONTROL FREAKS

Haman was definitely a Control Freak. "He is devoured by this obsession with control," writes Michael V. Fox in *Character and Ideology in the Book of Esther*. "Mordecai's refusal to show fear, indeed his very presence at the King's Gate, proves to Haman that, whatever he might think, he lacks control. He cannot govern the Jew's emotions; he cannot even prevent his current presence in the place of power. But ironically and appropriately, this obsession with control in effect imposes Mordecai's presence upon all of his thoughts and gives Mordecai power over his mind, robbing him of all pleasure he might derive from the honor, wealth, and power in which he glories."

Marie, a manager at a large cosmetics company, works for a modern-day Control Freak. "My boss is always hovering over my shoulder and second guessing everything I do. She insists that everything be done her way—even when my way works just as well, or even better."

These hands-on micromanagers are typically perfectionists. They over-supervise, hoard information, and often delegate tasks to their subordinates, but rarely the responsibility or authority to accomplish those tasks. Their philosophy: "No one can do it as well as I can."

Insecurity and fear of failure are the driving forces behind a Control Freak's persistent meddling. "On the plus side, these bosses tend to be very conscientious, take their responsibilities seriously, and are dedicated and hard-working," says Reed Moskowitz, M.D., medical director of the Stress Disorders Center at New York University Medical Center, where bad bosses are a common complaint.

Control Freaks are generally not dangerous—as Haman was—but they can definitely drive you nuts trying to achieve your—and their—goals. To stay sane and keep a Control Freak off your back, your best bet is to:

Think of this type of boss as an overprotective parent. "The best way to deal with a Control Freak is to drown her in information," says Dr. Moskowitz. "The more you give and the less she has to worry about, the more she'll let go."

Resist overtly fighting your boss's suffocating ways. This is the worst thing you can do," Dr. Moskowitz insists, because bucking this type of boss sets off an alarm. "The boss may think, 'This person is not a team player, this person won't take supervision, this person is trying to hide something.'"

Reassure the Control Freak that you're on his side while simultaneously asserting your own work style. "I once counseled a manager whose boss was sending her long memos directing her movements," says New York City career coach and assertive-training specialist Hilda Meltzer, MSE. "I encouraged the manager to speak with her boss privately and say, 'You know, I work very well on my own. When I get memos exhorting me to do things a certain way, I feel it's counterproductive. I know what a track record you have, and I'm here to support you, but I can produce best with more autonomy.'"

Always deliver. Hand in everything on time—and when you do, point out that you've met your boss's deadline and conformed to her specifications. If you consistently do what you say, when you say you'll do it, a Control Freak is likely to back off or go away and bother somebody less reliable.

Coping with Cutthroats

They're slick, sneaky, and more often than not, sleazy. With their Jekyll-and-Hyde personalities, Cutthroats may appear to be your staunchest supporters—to your face. But turn around, and they're likely to stab you in the back by badmouthing you or stealing your ideas.

Most Cutthroats are incompetent, but they manage to maintain power by lying, manipulating, working the office grapevine, and playing people off one another. They are also known to kiss up to their superiors while mistreating their subordinates. Many lack integrity and have a tendency to be unethical as well—particularly if this kind of behavior serves their purpose.

How to cope with a Cutthroat? Here's some advice:

Let your boss know you're on to him. Remember how the tables turned when Queen Esther pointed the finger at Haman? Sometimes all it takes to make a Cutthroat back off is a private one-on-one conversation in which you make it crystal clear that you won't stand for his lying and manipulating ways.

Many women cringe at any suggestion of conflict, choosing, instead, to avoid confrontation at all costs. But if the Cutthroat you work for has been stealing your ideas or blaming his mistakes on you, you have no choice—your career is on the line! "You've got to confront, stick to the issues, and document your actions," says Dr. Moskowitz.

How to best do that? He advises sticking with the facts. "Use polite, respectful but firm language. Review what's happened and discuss it in an open-ended way by saying, 'This is the experience I had, these are the facts as I understood them, and this is the position I felt I was in.'"

"If your boss is honest, he will admit there was a mistake or a misperception," adds Dr. Moskowitz. "This will clear the air, and it shouldn't happen again. But if it does happen repeatedly and your boss's behavior continues, then you have to realize you're dealing with somebody who has no ethics, no morals, no values—and you have to ask yourself if you really want to be in that situation."

Find a way to bypass a Cutthroat's devious ways. Meltzer recalls a client who got an undeserved poor performance evaluation from a Cutthroat she worked for, who couldn't deal with his subordinate's outstanding track record. "This manager was so insulted by the evaluation that she decided to take action," Meltzer reports.

"First, she considered going above her boss's head. But she knew that strategy probably wouldn't work, as this Cutthroat had somehow managed to make himself quite valuable to top management. So, she decided, instead, to prove her value in a visible manner through her performance."

"She set about developing a special project that was so successful, she was sent around the country to give reports on it," Meltzer continues. "This brought visibility to herself and her department, and ultimately, she earned high praise from top management. It took a year, but she proved indirectly that the evaluation couldn't hold water, and her Cutthroat boss retreated."

Get in the habit of protecting your ideas. When you have a really good one, make sure to share it with your boss in front of someone else. Even if he claims not to like it, he won't be able to pass it off as his own later on, since both of you will know that others heard you. Better yet, bring your ideas up at meetings and include them in handouts that you pass around to all in attendance. That way, everyone (including your boss) has documentation on who the brainchild behind the idea really is.

Determine if moving on might be your best option. "I think Cutthroats are the toughest of all the bad bosses to deal with," says Dr. Moskowitz. "They have all kinds of excuses, all types of rationalizations. They'll try to turn things around and say it's your problem, that you did the wrong thing, that you didn't understand."

Peggy, who recently made a lateral move at the financing company where she works, agrees. "My former boss wasn't a bad person—he just wasn't up to the job and basically was given it because he'd been around for so long and was next in line. But whenever he had to make a decision, he would delegate it to me. Then if things went well, he didn't hesitate to take credit for it all in front of our superiors. When there were problem, however, I was always the scapegoat. Finally, I had to leave and make a fresh start."

TAMING A TYRANT

Haman was the ultimate Tyrant: explosive and demeaning, hard-nosed and demanding. Unfortunately, in modern times, there appear to be plenty of bosses somewhat like him still hanging around. In fact, Harvey Hornstein, Ph.D., author of *Brutal Bosses and Their Prey*, estimates that a whopping 90 percent of us have worked for a Tyrant. His conclusions are based on a survey of nearly 1,000 workers over eight years.

These bosses are typically manipulative and mean spirited. They can even be verbally abusive, as many derive a sense of power and importance by publicly humiliating others. Listen in to a handful of victims' tales . . .

My boss has a short fuse and gets a kick out of berating me in front of everyone. At staff meetings, he often puts me down with comments like, "Can't you do anything right?" or "I can't believe you made that mistake again." Once, he even brought a dunce cap for me to wear.

In my last job, the new ad manager made it clear she didn't like me. This was probably because I was really good at my job—I was the top seller in my office for

three years straight—and because I had strong relationships with my colleagues. Whenever we'd meet to discuss sales quotas, she'd take personal phone calls and
talk forever, and once when I asked for a raise, she
laughed at me. Personally, I think she was jealous of my
popularity in the office and felt threatened by me because she thought I wanted her job.

My boss is a workaholic who plays favorites, ignores suggestions and tries to pit coworkers against one another
thinking that will make us all work harder. It doesn't.

When I defended a colleague my boss was yelling at in
the hallway outside her office, I became the next target
for abuse. Immediately, my boss started refusing to share
critical information with me on deadlines and productivity goals. He also started giving me and my subordinates conflicting instructions on major projects.

The bad news: The numbers of bully bosses in today's workplace appear to be on the rise. What gives? Hornstein attributes
much of this to the pressures bosses are under due to rampant
restructurings and downsizings. "Feeling powerless, bosses en-
force their power over others; feeling small, they belittle others
in the futile hope that it will make them appear big." In other
words, as organizations get leaner, more and more bosses get
meaner.

The good news: It's not so difficult to avoid power struggles
with a Tyrant and succeed in spite of their nasty behavior. If you
work for a Tyrant, here's how to erect a bully barrier:

Learn to ignore your boss's desperate behaviors. That's how Queen Esther dealt with Haman when he fell at her feet, begging for his life. Granted, this may sound like a copout, but "if you ignore by choice, it's not cowardice; it's being assertive," says Meltzer. Besides, when Tyrants rant and rave, and you respond by cowering or losing your cool, this plays right into their hands, assuring them that they are powerful and in control. "When these bosses know they can get to you, they will," confirms Robert Bramson, author of *Coping with Difficult Bosses*. "But the flip side is also true. When they know they *can't* get to you, they won't bother."

Try defusing his anger by asking questions. Keep in mind that if a Tyrant has lost control, it usually means he's feeling insecure. You can help him chill, focus, and get back to the business at hand by asking questions: "What's the problem here?" "What needs to be done right now?" "How can I help?" This subtly reassures the Tyrant that he's the boss. It also reminds him that you're on his side, and that you're both working toward mutual goals.

Separate the message from the medium. Suppose the Tyrant has humiliated you in front of your colleagues or said some nasty things to you in private. His behavior may be inexcusable, but is his message justified? In other words, behind the tantrums or sarcasm, does he have good reason to complain about you or your work? Be honest with yourself.

Stand up to abuse. There will be situations where you can't bite your tongue—and you shouldn't have to. But how to respond to a Tyrant's vicious personal attacks? Calmly tell your boss, "I am a professional. I will not tolerate you talking to me like this. I expect you to treat me like a professional—with

ROYAL ADVICE

I've held the same job for nearly 25 years and love every minute of it. That is, until my beloved boss recently retired. Unfortunately, his replacement is impossible to work for. The problem? No matter what I do, I can't please him. He gives me vague directions, then rants and raves when I do something wrong. And when I do something right, he never offers any praise. I'm two years short of retirement myself. Any tips for hanging on until then?

If you enjoy your work, feel challenged and are happy with your contributions, don't let a bad boss rain on your parade. If you think there's a chance of improving your relationship with your boss, by all means, give it your best shot. Schedule a meeting with him and tell him matter-of-factly, "I'm concerned that you feel my work often falls short of your expectations. To help me meet your goals, could we talk at greater length when you give me an assignment, or schedule weekly meetings to review my progress?"

If this strategy doesn't work, realize that you're probably not going to change him. You can, however, change how you react to him by simply detaching yourself—even feeling sorry for him. And that can make an impossible boss more tolerable.

courtesy and without putting me down or yelling." According to Jeffrey Caponigro, author of *The Crisis Counselor*, "When you do this, bullies often back down because they recognize that you won't be a victim who will let them get away with their antics."

Document everything. Save vicious memos, print out nasty e-mails, and write down every insult your bully boss hurls your way—just in case you need to share all these with human resources should a Tyrant try to oust you from your job.

BEWARE: TOXIC BOSSES

There's another kind of superior that disturbs women like Margaret Heffernan, president and COO for iCast, the most. She calls these bosses "toxic." "Toxic bosses claim to like women," she writes in an article for *Fast Company*. "But they like them strictly as ornaments, not as power players. Toxic bosses aren't overly sexist, and they're not impossible to work for. But they do poison the atmosphere and pollute the environment. And they do create alienating, macho cultures in which it's tough for women to have much fun. Somehow, they can never quite get over the feeling that women in business are charming, submissive, fun to have around, and nice as eye candy—but never quite 'one of us.' "

Heffernan is all too familiar with toxic bosses, having spent more than ten years running five businesses both in the United States and the United Kingdom. "For years, I was the only female CEO at CMGI," she says. "But it wasn't until I read the company's proxy statement that I realized my salary was 50 percent of that of my male counterparts. I had the CEO title, but I was being paid as if I were a director."

Throughout her career, Heffernan has been the victim of sexual stereotyping countless times. "At one of the companies I ran, a core part of my job was to negotiate agreements with the labor unions. One of the union bosses took me out to lunch at a Chinese restaurant and used the opportunity to order the most gruesome items on the menu: webbed chicken feet, ducks' tongues, lambs' testicles. The challenge was obvious—and I rose to it. But where I used to tell this story with pride, I now realize that, in a way, I fell into his trap. A far better response to his test would have been to simply order my own dishes, food that I preferred. I should have refused to do the guy thing."

Toxic bosses are the reason why women are leaving big companies as fast as they can, Heffernan believes. "By 2005, there will be about 4.7 million self-employed women in the United States, up 77 percent since 1983. The increase for men? Just six percent. Women leave because they want to work differently and because they don't want to have to add the second job of becoming a change agent to their existing job. Women don't want to redecorate the company. They want to build something new, different, and theirs—from scratch."

Avoiding Catfights in the Office

A mere handful of women currently sit at the helm of America's largest corporations. What's holding competent, capable women back? Toxic bosses? Certainly. The glass ceiling? Most definitely. But here's another obstacle women fact that's likely to surprise you.

In their book *In the Company of Women: Turning Workplace Conflicts into Powerful Alliances*, authors Pat Heim, Susan Murphy, and Susan K. Golant suggest that frustrated female employees should also point the finger at women they work with for keeping them out of the executive suite.

In fact, Heim, who has run workshops for women in business titled "How to Survive in a Male World," reports that participants didn't seem to think that men were the ones holding them back. "They'd say, 'yeah, that's true, but women are the real problem.'"

A recent poll conducted by *Oxygen* Media concurs: 65 percent of women said they resent other women who are either in power or act like they are. "Most working women are quick to acknowledge that among female co-workers, there is sufficient backbiting, gossip, and other indirect acts of aggression to thwart women on their path to success," reports Murphy.

Why wouldn't women go all out to support and boost one another to top positions? The authors have this theory about what typically goes wrong: "Women become close in the workplace, and when friendships between female colleagues go sour, they can wreak havoc in the office. Men do not have this problem, because they tend to be more reserved with one another at work."

Positive workplace relationships are definitely important in the world of women, and according to organizational psychologist Carol Gallagher, they are also central to our dealings in the business world. When writing *Going to the Top*, Gallagher found that the ability to maintain positive relationships was among the four critical success factors in the careers of 200 high-ranking senior executives she studied. "The ability to develop relationships is imperative in crossing the threshold to the next level," she writes.

Unfortunately, however, when women do get noticed and promoted, their success is often jeered—rather than cheered—by their female coworkers. Sheryl's story is a perfect example.

"Last year, my boss volunteered me to coordinate our company's summer picnic, which is a really big deal," says the 36-year-old senior claims manager at a large Miami insurance firm. "I was super-swamped at the time and didn't want to do it. But I was flattered to be asked and figured accepting the challenge might win me some brownie points in terms of visibility."

The picnic was a huge success, and all of the company's head honchos were impressed. As a result, Sheryl's boss began giving her plum assignments and grooming her for a promotion. "Naturally, I was thrilled, but my coworkers were not," she says. "Many made jokes or snide comments about my good fortune. They started referring to me as the 'boss's pet' and giving me the cold shoulder. Fewer and fewer of my so-called friends dropped by my office to chat, and I was rarely invited to lunch or after-work get-togethers. I felt hurt, but what made matters even worse was that after the promotion went through, I had to supervise some of these women, and many of them were less than cooperative. Dealing with the personal snubs was something I could handle, but dealing with their attitudes was tougher. I was really worried about not being able to do a good job."

Sound familiar? If you've ever been singled out for a plum assignment or advanced beyond your coworkers, you can understand Sheryl's predicament. Almost all catfighting in the office can be chalked up to jealous coworkers, whose childish behavior can definitely hold you back, says nationally certified career counselor Susanne Beier, president of Susanne Parente Associates. How to prevent resentful coworkers from sabotaging your success? Try these tips.

Play down your good fortune. When you're the recipient of accolades from higher-ups, get handed a great project to oversee, or land a promotion, it's fine to be excited. "But too much enthusiasm can be misinterpreted as gloating," cautions Beier. "Don't belittle what you're doing, however. Acting like a 'victim' will come across as obviously insincere."

Remember the "power dead even" rule. Having to supervise friends is almost always a challenge for women. That's because while men typically have no qualms functioning in a hierarchy, women expect other women—regardless of their rank—to behave as if they have equal power. "This is what I call the rule of 'power dead even,'" says Heim.

"Getting promoted sends a woman's workplace relationships out of whack," she explains. "Her good buddies will say, 'She's drunk with power,' 'Who does she think she is,' and 'She's a bitch,' even if the newly promoted woman hasn't done anything except give someone an assignment."

Share in the "grunt" work. Just because you have new responsibilities—or even an new job—doesn't mean you can't help out in a crunch. "It will make life easier for you in the long run if you do," Beier says. "Your coworkers will see that they haven't lost a 'team member.'"

Continue to reach out to office pals. They may withdraw from you—at least initially—but if you pull away, it will only intensify the rifts. So, find time to play catch-up during coffee breaks or lunch. "If *you* behave normally, eventually people around you will, too," Beier says.

Don't be afraid to confront problem coworkers. On a *Good Morning America* segment, Karen Catchpole, a senior editor at *Jane* magazine, shared the story of a former female coworker who she says "actively resented me and who wouldn't listen to my ideas or act on my ideas. One day, I walked into the conference room after a meeting that we'd all had, and I found a piece of paper that someone had obviously left behind. I picked it up and looked at it. It said, 'things that annoy me about Karen.'"

Catchpole's reaction? "I stuck a Post-it note with the words, 'you dropped this' written on the offending paper, then folded the paper and placed it on the female colleague's desk. It was never spoken of, which I think was a big mistake."

Heim agrees. "A better idea would have been to confront the woman in a positive ways, saying something like, 'I found this note, and I think we need to talk about it.' But women, who are raised to be indirect and avoid confrontation, don't do this—and that kind of behavior gets in the way of business."

Do all you can to rack up "chips" with colleagues. Chips? In their book, Heim, Murphy, and Galant talk about the "Chip Theory," which is basically a token system all women use—often unknowingly. Each of us is endowed with a certain number of chips of power—positive attributes or actions—that we constantly exchange with others, they explain. And we all possess, give, and get these power chips in three ways: through pleasant interactions with others (like telling someone, "Great job landing the XYZ account," asking how someone's vacation was, or remembering someone's birthday with a card); by birthright (those born into wealth or blessed with good looks, talent, intelligence, etc. generally have more chips); and through active acquisition (by obtaining an MBA or Ph.D., by marrying someone handsome or rich, etc.).

"Although you may not have been aware of it until now, everyone with whom you interact keeps a chip bankbook on you," the authors say. "All day long, you are gaining and losing chips with your subordinates, peers, and higher-ups. They know where you stand with them at any given moment, and you know where they stand with you."

One of the most important rules in the Chip Theory is that "we always make it equal in the end—that is, if someone tries to take away our chips, we will find a way to even the score." Conversely, the opposite is true. Racking up chips by doing nice things

ROYAL ADVICE

I recently landed my first management job at a large insurance company. Thus far, I think I'm making great progress at winning the respect and cooperation of my subordinates. There are a couple of women, however, who are twenty years older than me and who are trying to undermine everything I do. I heard that one of them applied for my job, so she's probably upset that I was chosen over her. What steps can I take to win these women over?

When you're the new boss—and a young one at that—there will always be people less than thrilled with your appointment. After all, your career is racing ahead faster than theirs, and at an earlier age. Consequently, they may resent having to report to you. They may also resist your ideas or try to patronize you.

Your best bet for earning these employees' respect and cooperation is to treat them as valuable resources of information on everything from company history to corporate politics. And that involves tapping them for their expertise as often as possible.

Other forms of flattery can work to your advantage as well. Compliment their efforts, praise them in front of others and never waste an opportunity to tell them how valuable they are to the company—and to you.

for others can work to your advantage when you have to confront someone. "In other words, if you have a chip surplus and have to have a difficult discussion, it's easier to manage," the authors add.

Share the glory. "Look for chances when coworkers can step in and show off their own work," advises Beier. "Praise them in front of the boss and in their presence. The more you help others shine, the better you will look."

Knowing When It's Time to Move On

Bad bosses and back-stabbing colleagues are enough to make anyone want to update her résumé and call a headhunter. And sometimes quitting may be your best option. Tempting as it may be to hang in there, sometimes circumstances just aren't going to get any better, and by sticking around, you could be stalling your career.

Gwen Simmons, former director of the Counseling and Testing Center at the University of North Carolina-Pembroke, recalls quitting a teaching job early in her career "when my boss, the school's principal, was disrespectful to students and seemed to enjoy embarrassing low achievers. I knew it was time to move on when 30 out of 33 faculty signed a petition asking that he be removed—but he was allowed to return."

Before making a decision to leave, however, you need to figure out whether you're dealing with a bad boss or a bad person. In other words, you can often teach a bad boss to be a better boss. But a bad person—someone who's cruel, vicious, and evil, like Haman—that's a different story. In such cases, there's usually just one answer: the exit door.

In 1994, Candace Kaspers, former chairperson of the communications department at Kennesaw University in Marietta,

Georgia, raised concerns of anti-Semitism over her dean's proposed plan to replace the department's only two Jewish instructors. A day after objecting to the reorganization plan, she was asked to resign her chairmanship. Rather than accept a demotion, she chose to resign.

Three years later, Kaspers, who is not Jewish, won a $275,000 judgment in court for retaliatory discrimination. Later, she dropped a reinstatement bid in exchange for a $750,000 settlement and launched her own diversity-consulting business. "Standing up for your principles rather than accepting a superior's flawed moves increases your value and credibility," she believes.

Other signs that it may be time to leave? As a rule of thumb, you should consider looking for a new job if:

You're being kept out of the information loop. How can you do your job properly if you're not getting the information you need? This is a typical power play, and signs this is happening include: Your boss or coworkers "forget" to invite you to important meetings, to copy you on memos, or to e-mail you regarding an important issue.

You're not getting the plum assignments. Or a pet project of yours is approved but is assigned to one of your colleagues. If you have no opportunity to shine, what's the point in sticking around?

Your boss intimidates you. Has his verbal abuse gotten to be more than you can handle? Maybe at first, you thought you could change him; now you know you never will. So, why work for someone who's never going to support your upward mobility?

On the flip side, however, there are definite benefits to hanging tough. "You learn to deal with frustration, navigate a war zone, and in the case of a problem boss, how to manage upwards," says

Brian Stern, president of Shaker Consulting Group, a management consulting firm. Plus, if you succeed in spite of these obstacles, people who matter are bound to notice, and survival could be your stepping-stone to the top.

Janet's story should inspire you. After surviving 18 months with a Tyrant, this executive in a large manufacturing company was "rescued" by one of her company's main competitors. "Everyone in the industry knew what a monster my boss was. People would always ask me, 'How do you manage to stay so cool?' In retrospect, I think I went out of my way to be cordial with others *because* my boss was so rude, plus I was totally dedicated to doing all I could to keep profits up. Sure, I tried confronting my boss privately, but mostly I learned to ignore him. And I never uttered an unkind word about him to anyone—except maybe my husband."

Janet's sense of professionalism, loyalty, and dedication paid off. "At a trade show, the CEO from a competing company invited me to lunch and offered me a job," she reports. "He said he figured that if I could last 18 months with my existing boss—and still manage to do a good job—I'd probably stay with him forever. He may be right. That was six years ago—and I'm still here!"

Sticking around also enables you to make a difference, be a change agent—which was exactly why Margaret Heffernan opted to stay at a company where she was underpaid and subjected to absurd, sexist stereotypes. Like Esther, she made a selfless decision.

"I had enough autonomy to create a different kind of culture for all of the people who worked for me," she says. "I believe women genuinely long for the opportunity to create different structures and different cultures where people can thrive—places where men and women alike can stop taking it and instead unleash their hearts and minds on businesses that respect their capabilities, their commonalties, and their differences."

TAKE HEART!

Whether you choose to stay or leave, keep your spirits high by reminding yourself that things could be worse. To write *Best Boss, Worst Boss*, James Miller sponsored a contest inviting workers to submit horror stories of managers—and he came up with a slew of Haman-like doozies. Winning entries included:

- The tightwad who cut costs by separating two-ply tissue in order to make two rolls from one for the employee bathroom.
- The Scrooge who handed out moldy food and expired-date canned goods as Christmas bonuses.
- The manager who forbade his employees to summon help after an elderly coworker suffered a fatal heart attack at his desk. 'He didn't want anyone to dial 911 until five o'clock, because he said it would disrupt work for the rest of the day—and the guy was dead anyway," says Miller.

So, take heart, watch your back, have the strength, patience and persistence of Esther, and you *will* prevail! ♔

8

KEEPING THE FAITH

*E*sther's life was filled with hurdles. As a young Jewish girl, she was taken—against her will—from a comfortable home and loving family to live in the king's palace as part of his harem. Soon after, she was considered for—and named—queen, a position she neither wanted nor aspired to.

Esther harbored a dangerous secret as well—that she was Jewish—and was forced the keep the special relationship she had with her beloved cousin Mordecai under wraps. Ultimately, she even had to risk her life—by facing off against the wicked Haman—to save her people from destruction.

But by keeping the faith and remaining true to her principles, Esther persevered and prospered . . .

That day, King Ahasuerus gave Queen Esther the estate of Haman, persecutor of the Jews. And Mordecai came into the presence of the king, for Esther had told how he was related to her. The king took off his signet ring, which he had reclaimed from Haman, and presented it to Mordecai. And Esther appointed him over Haman's estate.
—*Esther 8:1–3*

The evil Haman had been hanged, but Esther still had unfinished business with the king . . .

Falling at his feet and weeping, Esther begged the king to
put an end to the evil plan of Haman the Agagite, which
he had devised against the Jews. Then the king extended
the gold scepter to Esther and she arose and stood before
him. "If it pleases the king," she said, "and if he regards
me with favor and thinks it is the right thing to do, and if
he is pleased with me, let an order be written overruling
the dispatches that Haman devised and wrote to destroy
the Jews in all the king's provinces. For how can I bear to
see disaster fall on my people? How can I bear to see the
destruction of my family?"
—*Esther 8:3–6*

*The king was more than happy to grant his wife's wish, but
there was one problem. By law, once the king had signed an order, it
could not be revoked. Still, the king had an idea, which he proposed
to Esther and Mordecai . . .*

"Now write another decree in the king's name in behalf
of the Jews as seems best to you, and seal it with the
king's signet ring—for no document written in the king's
name and sealed with his ring can be revoked."
—*Esther 8:8*

*The royal secretaries were summoned at once to write out these
new orders, which were immediately dispatched to every Jew in all
of the king's 127 provinces . . .*

The king's edict granted the Jews in every city the right
to assemble and protect themselves, to destroy, kill and
annihilate any armed force of any nationality or province
that might attack them and their women and children;
and to plunder the property of their enemies. The day
appointed for the Jews to do this in all the provinces of
King Ahasuerus was the thirteenth day of the twelfth

month, the month of Adar. A copy of the text of the edict
was to be issued in every province and made known to
the people of every nationality so that the Jews would be
ready on that day to avenge themselves on their enemies.
—*Esther 8:11–13*

*Now all Esther and Mordecai could do was wait, and hope, and
pray that their plan would be successful.*

Oswald Chambers, author of several books on spirituality,
once said, "A crisis does not make character; a crisis reveals character"—and at this point in her life, Esther's character has never
shined brighter.

Think about it. Considering the obstacles she faced, Esther
could easily have become angry and bitter. After all, as queen
wasn't she entitled to a life of peace, and quiet, and luxury? Safely
sequestered in the palace, she could have easily chosen to ignore
Mordecai's pleas to use her power to save the Jews. And she certainly could have opted not to jeopardize her own life by approaching the king, unsummoned, and exposing Haman.

Instead, Esther chose to follow her conscience, to do the
"right thing." She took a huge leap of faith, and by doing so, revealed her strength of character. Moreover, by rising above all of
the adversity she faced, Esther emerged stronger and more powerful than ever.

Was this her destiny? Perhaps. Rewind her story back to where
Mordecai was attempting to persuade Esther to go to the king.
"Who knows?" he said. "Perhaps you have come to royal dignity for
just such as time as this."

In ancient times—and still today—there are many who believe
that things happen for a reason. Call it fate, a sense of providence,

divine intervention. Or, maybe it's true that some higher power places certain people in certain places at certain times—as a learning experience or even as a test to see how well they will fare.

If so, Esther triumphed. She dug deep for courage. She tapped inner strengths she never knew she had. She had unshakable faith. And by viewing herself not as a victim but as a change agent, she not only endured but inspired.

THE ESTHER EFFECT

Faced with modern-day obstacles, setbacks, and crises, could you do the same? Key to answering that question is how you typically handle diversity. Do you give up, or do you fight? Do you fall into the victim trap, or do you come out scarred but stronger? Do you cave into frustration, or do you summon the faith to rebound? Do you look for someone or something to blame, or do you stay focused on the high ground ahead? Do you collapse, or do you ride it out and move forward?

If you want to be like Esther, you must find the strength and courage to emerge as a powerful force both in your own life and the lives of others. The ability, drive, and determination to do this is what Dianna Booher calls the "Esther Effect"—or the impact you have when you are placed in a situation in which you can encourage or influence others, or change the course of events.

"And your biggest opportunity to have the 'Esther Effect' could be your strong character in handling adversity, hurt, and disappointments in your life," she writes in *The Esther Effect: The Seven Secrets of Self-Confidence and Influence.*

Read on for some remarkably courageous tales of modern-day Queen Esthers who personify this effect—and whose ultimate triumphs will help guide you through any trying and troubled times you face . . .

"Making Lemonade from Lemons"

Many young girls dream of becoming doctors when they grow up. "I'll be rich. I'll be important. I can help—even save—people," they imagine. But when young Jamie Weisman decided to become a doctor, she had a more compelling reason: to help herself.

At the age of 15, Weisman began her battle against a mysterious and painful illness that doctors couldn't seem to pinpoint. Its symptoms: bizarre ailments and unusual infections. For example, in her early twenties, her parotid gland got infected and her entire face swelled. "It was horribly painful to eat—each bite of food caused the infected gland to contract, as if someone were tightening a bolt in my face tighter and tighter, until the bone was about to shatter," she recalls. "I had no ideas what was causing this pain, but I adapted. I wore my hair down to hide the swelling. And since it hurt to eat, I didn't eat."

It took 11 years for Weisman to be diagnosed with a rare immune deficiency syndrome that to this day causes her daily discomfort—plus makes her susceptible to everything from painful infections to cancer. But with a diagnosis came treatment options and the chance to live a more normal life.

Before that, Weisman was constantly ill with infections—"from sepsis to shingles. By age 26, I'd had three operations, four lymph nodes removed, and five bone-marrow biopsies. I'd been called a hypochondriac by my boss and been told by a hematologist that in all likelihood, I had or would soon have cancer. I had visited doctors from Minnesota to Massachusetts seeking an explanation for my disease."

At last, Weisman was started on a protocol she currently follows. "I give myself injections [of interferon] at home every other night before I go to bed. Next to the alarm clock and the lamp and whatever book I'm reading, there are a few syringes and alcohol pads so I won't forget my shots. And once a month, I go to the infusion room at the Emory Clinic [in Atlanta] to get intravenous infusions of gammaglobin, or my 'juice,' as my nurse, Sarah, calls it."

This infusion takes about three hours and has been Weisman's monthly ritual for the last eight years. "I expect it will be for the rest of my life," she says. Indeed, her disease, while treatable, has no known cure.

Throughout her perilous journey, however, Weisman has demonstrated remarkable courage. In fact, along the way, she decided to become a doctor herself. It was her way of "making lemonade out of lemons," of gaining a better understanding of the body that betrayed her, and of gaining control instead of relinquishing it.

Weisman's decision to go to medical school surprised her family and doctors, who were concerned about the risks to her health, including stress and exposures to infection. But they needn't have worried. Weisman sailed through medical school and even managed to begin writing a book about her experiences, which she finished during her residency. *As I Live and Breathe* is a memoir full of hope and everyday humor that "felt good to write because with writing, you sort out a lot of your emotions," she says.

Despite her illness, Weisman, who is married and the mother of two, strives to lead a normal life. "I ride my mountain bike, work out on a Stairmaster (though not as often as I ought to), sleep late on Sundays and read the paper in bed with my dog curled up at my feet," she writes. However, chronic pain—and those monthly visits to the infusion room in particular—are a constant reminder of her illness.

Indeed, each time that IV needle pierces her skin, Weisman flinches—but not from pain. "It's always when I feel the prick of the needle that the 'why me' thoughts come," she admits.

Faith and family have pulled her through this ordeal, she says. What's more, those hours spent receiving the antibodies she needs to stay alive and well have not only given her the courage to carry on, but have shaped her into the caring and compassionate doctor she has become.

"The gathering of patients in the infusion room forms a sort of de facto therapy group, a place where we can share the burdens of our conditions without hurting family members or feeling that we are taking up too much of our doctors' time. In the infusion room, we're all on equal footing. We all know what it feels like to be put to sleep for surgery and that horrible sensation of waking up from anesthesia, a stranger calling your name, your body convulsing with the tube pulled out from your throat. We know the post-operative confusion; we've been seen naked by nurses and doctors. We know what it is to wait for biopsy results, to argue with insurance companies, to get sick from medication and have to take it anyway. These are the things we discuss while we eat sandwiches and listen to CNN and swap gardening tips and movie reviews."

Having been a lifetime patient herself has also improved the way Weisman interacts with—and even diagnoses—her own patients. "My monthly trips to the Infusion Center have been as essential to my medical education as any course in anatomy or physiology," she says. "And the patients I have met there have educated me. I know illness from the inside out. I can take my experience and turn it around. I can treat my patients the way I would want to be treated."

"It's How You Respond"

Like many entrepreneurs, Lois Benjamin-Bohm and her Israeli husband, Shlomo, started their Manhattan-based moving business, Shleppers, on a shoestring budget. "We borrowed money to buy a used van and spent $12 on business cards," she says. Never mind that the couple had no moving experience, little business know-how, and no financial backing. They had chutzpah. They had each other. They had faith and determination to succeed.

"Initially, we walked up and down the streets with our infant son in the Snugli handing out business cards to all the store-keepers," Benjamin-Bohm recalls. Their business took off almost instantly, "Shleppers is such a New York name, and everyone could identify with it," she suspects.

Over the next ten years, their family grew (to three children), and so did Shleppers—to a million-dollar business. A fleet of trucks had replaced their secondhand van. "Every time I had a baby, we bought another truck," Benjamin-Bohm laughs. And while the couple worked side by side, it was Shlomo who was in charge of operations, while Lois handled administrative tasks and advertising.

All that changed on December 23, 1988, when Benjamin-Bohm's life was turned upside down. Her husband had taken the kids to visit relatives in Israel, while she stayed home to mind the store. "I remember the day as if it were yesterday," she says. "I had this strange awful feeling about my family. So, I picked up the phone to call my cousin in Israel to see how everyone was enjoying their vacation." It was after midnight there, and a sleepy baby-sitter who answered the phone assured Benjamin-Bohm that the kids were okay. But, gripped by a mysterious panic, she dialed a family friend in Israel.

Apprehensive as she was, nothing could have prepared her for what her friend revealed: "Lois, get on a plane. Your family is dead!"

All four, plus her cousin's son, had died when the car her husband was driving crashed head-on with a bus on a darkened road. Stunned, Benjamin-Bohm grabbed the last two seats for herself and a friend on a packed holiday flight and headed for Israel. "It's an eleven-hour plane ride, and the entire time I kept thinking, 'I can't believe everybody is killed. It can't be that everyone is dead.'"

Two weeks and one massive funeral later, Benjamin-Bohm returned to New York—reeling and relying on the support of family and counselors to get by. But she never asked, "Why me?" "Asking why is the wrong question," she insists. "You'll never learn the answer. Besides, it's not what happens to you, it's how you respond."

Determined not to let her tragedy consume her, Benjamin-Bohm decided to hold on to the family business and run it single-handedly. "So much of what I had built for the last 10 years was gone. I had to maintain *something* that let me know that I had a life, and Shleppers was it. It became this powerful thing in my mind. It was like this icon, this symbol of my life, and so it became very precious. I had to really take care of it, treat it, and nurture it.

Her grief-stricken employees, while supportive of Benjamin-Bohm and dedicated to keeping the company going, weren't so confident she was capable of running Shleppers. "The first time I met with them and announced my intentions to take over, I could feel the mockery in the air. They didn't think a woman could run the business by herself. But I decided that I would prove them wrong."

During her first few weeks at the helm, grief numbed Benjamin-Bohm to the point that she could barely concentrate—and the business suffered. Over the next few months, the thought of quitting crossed her mind many times. But eventually she realized, "You have to make a choice somewhere to go forward. If you don't make that choice, you become a victim."

Slowly, business improved, and Shleppers recently celebrated its 25th anniversary—a milestone Benjamin-Bohm worked hard to reach. She has worked equally hard to rebuild her personal life without sacrificing her past. She established a scholarship fund at two Manhattan schools in her deceased children's names. She also got remarried—to a family friend who helped her through her ordeal—and she and her second husband have four children together, ages six to nine.

"I think of the husband and children I lost every single day. Not a day goes by that it's not there," she says. "But all of my personal life is just as good as my business. I've got a wonderful husband and four children. I'm happy. Life must go on."

"You Don't Get over It. You Don't Get through It. You Just Get to a Softer Place."

Linda Novey-White's tragic tale began when she was just six years old. Her father, a master electrician, received a severe shock and was hospitalized for four years. The family lost everything—including "the good house in the good neighborhood," Novey-White says.

When the family moved, the yard surrounding their new dwelling was barren and depressing—until the day Novey-White returned from school to find irises growing along the front walk.

"My mother had planted beauty in all that ugliness," says Novey-White, who has filled her own life with irises ever since, "as a symbol of hope."

Turns out, she would need plenty of them. At 19, Novey-White married a serviceman and enrolled in college. Over the next fourteen years, she attended "thirteen or fourteen colleges and earned 264 credits but no degree." She also had two children—both born with a rare and life-threatening kidney disorder. Then six months, into her third pregnancy, she developed uterine cancer. The child was born healthy, the cancer was caught early, and things were finally looking up.

But in 1972, the very year she was named "Military Wife of the Year," Novey-White's husband left her. With no bank account, no job experience, no degree, and three girls to raise, this resourceful single mom sold the family's furniture for cash, then loaded up the car and moved with her daughters to Panama City, Florida. There, they lived in a leaky, four-room beach house that her ex-husband had once given her for Mother's Day. "It had two cupboards, one closet, and a half-bath—but it was paid for," she laughs.

Somehow, Novey-White managed to turn her volunteer experience into a paying public relations job at Chase Development Corporation. "I was hired to handle marketing and public relations, but had no clue what that entailed," she recalls. "So, the day I was hired, I checked out 23 books from the library and gave myself a crash course."

In no time, Novey-White had found her niche: motivating people. In fact, she was so successful at motivating teams at work to sell residential developments, that a Florida magazine did a feature story on her. That, in turn, led to an invitation to speak at the

Florida Governor's Conference—and as luck would have it, presidents from United Airlines and Marriott Corporation were in the audience.

Blown away by her talk, these corporate head honchos offered her a job motivating and energizing their customer service staffs. But being a consultant meant extensive traveling, and Novey-White wanted to stay close to her young children.

Marriott Corporation founder and then-president J. W. Marriott wouldn't take no for an answer, however, and finally persuaded Novey-White that she could make more money as a consultant. In 1981, she launched Linda Novey Enterprises, and soon she was able to add four bedrooms and two baths to her Panama City house. She could also afford to plant plenty of irises.

Eleven years later, however, misfortune reared again when Novey-White's youngest daughter, who was planning her wedding, was killed in a car accident. "When Paula died, everything else paled in comparison," she says. "I thought, 'Nothing else that happens in my life will get me down. I've done it all now.'"

Days later, she found out she had melanoma.

In a strange way, this latest crisis helped to snap her out of her intense grief. Anxious to get back to work—"my salvation"— she knew she had to focus on getting healthy fast. "You don't get over it. You don't get through it. You just get to a softer place."

Indeed, the same year her 23-year-old daughter died, Novey-White remarried. She has since moved to Manatee, Florida, where she has a home office that's filled with flowers. Business is booming—with clients like Marriott, Ritz-Carlton, Nikko Hotels, and General Cinemas depending on her to train and motivate their customer service employees. And thanks to her unwavering can-do attitude—and plenty of irises—she has managed to keep the faith.

"This Is Not about Luck. This Is about God Having a Plan."

Since September 11, 2001, Genelle Guzman-McMillan has been haunted by one burning question: "Why me?" this softspoken 31-year-old office manager from Trinidad worked for the Port Authority on the 64th floor of the World Trade Center's North Tower. On September 11, she had just grabbed a bagel and turned on her computer when she felt the building sway. She rushed to the window and discovered to her horror, that a plane had hit the building. She then raced to find her closest colleague, Rosa Gonzalez. "We have to leave," the two agreed.

But not before making a couple of quick telephone calls to let relatives know they were okay. Gonzalez called her sister, and Guzman-McMillan left a message on her fiance's answering machine.

Minutes later, a second plane hit the South Tower, and the two women raced for the stairs. The pair had made it down 51 flights when the building began to collapse. "Everything was coming down," Guzman-McMillan recalls in an interview with *Essence* magazine. "It felt like an earthquake, hurricane, everything in one."

Indeed, the tumbling of the tower hurled Guzman-McMillan and Gonzalez into a wall. "My hand was still on Rosa's shoulder when the building started crumbling, then it just got dark. Rosa pulled away, and I got up from the corner where I fell and started to move away, too. Then something hit me. I got stuck right there, and I couldn't move anymore. And the building just started to crumble, faster and faster."

When everything stopped, Guzman-McMillan expected to hear sounds—"people moving, trying to get out," she says. Instead, it was eerily quiet. But miraculously, she was alive.

For 26 hours, Guzman-McMillan remained beneath the rubble—an agonizing ordeal both physically and mentally. Her entire right side was covered with mounds of concrete and steel that were impossible to move, and her right calf was crushed. Her left arm was free, however, enabling her to wipe the layers of thick chalky dust that had accumulated in her eyes, nose, and mouth. The pain was almost unbearable, but her mind was alert. So, she passed the time thinking of her 13-year-old daughter, her fiancé, and her deceased mother. But mostly, she prayed for a miracle.

Her prayers were answered when she heard the distant sound of a rescue worker. "I'm here!" she screamed as loud as she could.

"Do you see the light?" he asked—but she couldn't. With every ounce of strength she had left, Guzman-McMillan picked up a chunk of stone and banged it against the concrete above her. Twenty minutes later, she was rescued—the last of just four people caught in the rubble to be pulled out alive.

Following five weeks in the hospital and four operations on her crushed leg, Guzman-McMillan began to heal physically. Emotionally, however, there are lingering scars that will likely last a lifetime. People often remark how lucky she is, but Guzman-McMillan disagrees, crediting the fact that she survived to divine providence. "This is not about luck. This is about God having a plan," she insists. "And He will reveal it to me one day. I think God will give me a sign."

REBOUNDING FROM LIFE'S CRUEL BLOWS

Like Esther, these four women faced formidable obstacles and crises, yet they managed to maintain their faith and ultimately triumph.

How did they do it? How did they face each day? How do people facing extraordinary circumstances manage to get on with their lives?

They know what Esther knew.

Those who bounce back, for example, have faith in some meaning, purpose, or power larger than themselves. And, just like Esther, they survive—and often even manage to thrive—by tapping into this inner strength.

Not surprisingly, researchers are finding that spirituality plays an important role in recovering from adversity. "People who pray are healthier, calmer, and yes, more resilient, than people who don't," says Christopher Peterson, Ph.D., professor of psychology and director of clinical training at the University of Michigan. A study he conducted of 150 coronary bypass patients found that those who prayed were less depressed after surgery than those who did not.

Other studies have shown that people with some form of spiritual belief—not just religion—are often happier and more optimistic, most likely because spirituality promotes hope and offers social support.

Oftentimes, people who survive soul-shattering crises also make valiant attempts to turn their personal tragedies into something positive. It's a kind of antidote to their pain. In fact, research reveals that such gestures also help people bounce back quicker by bringing them comfort and a renewed sense of purpose.

Among notable women who have turned loss into action are Nancy Brinker, who launched the Susan G. Komen Foundation in memory of her sister, who died of breast cancer; Carolyn McCarthy, elected to Congress on a gun-control platform after a gunman killed her husband and wounded her son; and model Christy Turlington, whose antismoking crusade is the result of her father's death from lung cancer and her own recent diagnosis of emphysema.

Add to that list Linda Novey-White, who works with charities that fight kidney disease and who coaches and mentors low-income women who dream of starting their own enterprises. Include Lois Benjamin-Bohm as well, who not only has established a memorial scholarship fund in her deceased children's names, but whose movers routinely collect work clothing from customers and deliver it free to Dress for Success, a nonprofit group that helps low-income women outfit themselves for interviews and jobs.

Finally, those who bounce back best don't usually waste their breath asking, "Why me?" Instead, they understand the "Esther Effect"—that things may happen for a reason. Instead of looking back, they choose to look forward and typically respond to adversity by carrying on with courage and faith in the future.

Soon after her court victory over Holocaust denier David Irving, Deborah Lipstadt went to synagogue to give thanks. Ironically, it was Purim, and her eyes grew misty as she heard one particular portion of the Scroll of Esther read aloud: *Who knows? Perhaps you have come to royal dignity for just such a time as this.*

"I heard that, and it made me think: "Who knows if not for this very reason I got the education I got. I got the upbringing I got. I got the job I got," she told the *Jerusalem Post.* "Maybe we're all meant to do one something really significant. Nobody knows of it. Nobody sees it, but we're all meant to do something. And maybe this is the something I was meant to do."

The "Rules" of Resiliency

Not many of us have waged uphill battles as steep as those fought by Weisman, Benjamin-Bohm, Novey-White, Guzman-McMillan —or even Esther. But we've all faced setbacks and losses that have thrown us for a loop and left us reeling.

So, what separates people who manage to roll with the punches from those who let setbacks and failures flatten them? For years, researchers assumed that people either were born with specific traits that made them resilient or had been raised in environments in which money, good parents, and/or a good education made them tougher.

Now they know for sure this isn't true. In fact, groundbreaking new studies that focus on bouncing back from adversity reveal that no matter how hard the blow, we *all* have the capacity to rebound. In other words, resiliency is an *acquired* skill, and you, too, can survive and overcome crises and failures by mastering these strategies that are key to bouncing back:

Practice failing. Patricia O'Gorman, Ph.D., author of *Dancing Backwards in High Heels: How Women Master the Art of Resilience*, recommends deliberately looking for opportunities in which you could very well fall on your face. "Resilience develops in adverse situations," she explains. "If you're in an environment where nothing happens, you won't learn to be resilient."

In other words, don't let fear of failure keep you from shaking up your life once in a while. Look for challenges. Take risks. Soon you'll discover that bouncing back from little crises provides you with the training and coping skills you'll need to rebound from the big ones.

Lose the victim mentality. When things go wrong, it can be tempting to throw a pity party. "I'm such a loser." "Why does everything happen to me?" But people who overcome failure are

those who don't take it personally or who refuse to let their mis-
fortunes define who they are. "Resiliency is being able to stand in
your pain and feel it, yet know that's not all that you are," says
O'Gorman.

Katherine Russell Rich, who chronicled her ten-year battle
with cancer in *The Red Devil: To Hell with Cancer and Back*,
agrees. "Cancer is part of who I am, but it's not everything. I
could have either made the cancer my identity or broadened myself." She chose the later option. "I've developed a ton of other
interests so people wouldn't just think of me as a victim. I've
taken up biking. I've accepted writing assignments in India and
Indonesia. I've written a book. What do I have to lose? Cancer
made me ballsy, and I like that."

Learn to "fail forward." Recognize that every setback brings
you one step closer to success, says John C. Maxwell, author of
Failing Forward: Turning Mistakes into Stepping Stones for Success.
"What's more, if you learn something from every setback, you'll
soon find yourself doing more of what you do when you succeed—and less of what you do when you fail."

Andrea Sullivan's story is a perfect example. As a child, Sullivan
always knew what she wanted to do when she grew up: save the
world. And after graduating from the University of Pennsylvania—
becoming the first African-American woman in the nation to
earn a doctorate in sociology with a specialty in criminology—she
seemed well on her way to living her dream.

By age 28, she'd landed a prestigious job working as an
urban policy advisor in the areas of criminology and crime prevention for the secretary of Housing and Urban Development
(HUD). Perks of the job included getting to meet famous politi-
cians, including President Jimmy Carter. And her fat paycheck
enabled her to buy a nice four-bedroom brownstone, collect

ROYAL ADVICE

Three months ago, I was fired from a job—unfairly. My boss and I had totally different work styles and approaches to solving problems. Now that I have several promising interviews lined up, I'm faced with having to explain being terminated. Should I mention what happened on my résumé or in my cover letter? What should I say about my boss in the interview? Who do I give for a reference?

When it comes to damage control after being fired, the rules are fairly straightforward. No, you don't have to volunteer the fact that you were fired on your résumé or make a reference it to it in your cover letter. If you land an interview, there will be an opportunity to discuss your situation then. You aren't even obligated to bring up being fired in an interview, but don't lie about it if asked—and chances are you will be.

Be gracious and positive with your response: "It wasn't a good fit, and my boss and I agreed that it was best for me to move on. I'm grateful for the opportunity to explore jobs better suited for me." Then switch your focus to discussing why and how the position you're interviewing for would be a good fit.

Never, under any circumstances, should you say anything negative about your former employer. Not only is this unprofessional, but pointing fingers raises doubts about *you*.

As for references, see if a mentor, a high-level executive, or someone in human resources at your former company would feel comfortable discussing your strengths.

Alma Thomas artwork, and drive a red-and-white Mercedes. She also got engaged to be married.

But Sullivan was miserable. "HUD's idea of crime prevention was putting more locks on the doors," she told *Essence* magazine. "My idea was getting the elderly and young people to sit down and rap—to unlock doors. That was unheard of. I wasn't saving anyone. I wasn't saving the world."

Sullivan wasn't feeling so great, either. The stresses of her job had caused her acne to flare up, and she'd put on an extra thirty pounds. At the suggestion of a friend, she went to see a naturopath (a physician who uses natural remedies to fight illness and who prescribes lifestyle changes to prevent disease). That appointment turned out to be a life-changing experience. Not only did Sullivan's health do a quick turnabout, but the doctor so impressed her that she decided to "change the world" by becoming a naturopath herself. "Some things are meant to be," she remembers thinking at the time. "And if you open yourself to that spirit, it captures you."

Initially, Sullivan held on to her job at HUD and signed up for night classes at Howard University, focusing mainly on science courses. Her parents supported her endeavor 100 percent, but her fiancé discouraged the career change. A year and a half later, when Sullivan was accepted at Seattle's Bastyr University—one of only two naturopathic colleges in the nation at the time—she dumped her boyfriend, then sold her car and artwork and refinanced her house to finance the cross-country move.

Medical school was grueling, and between her second and third year, Sullivan decided to pack up and head home. What went wrong? Seattle's dreary weather, scarcity of African Americans, and acute homesickness, she says. "I never lost my vision, I was just so beaten that I knew I had to rest."

During her year-long sabbatical, Sullivan read about spirituality, participated in personal-growth workshops, and went on a seven-week pilgrimage with her church—to Jerusalem, Egypt, and Assisi. During that journey, her desire to help others returned with a vengeance. "I believed that naturopathic medicine was what I was supposed to be doing," she says, "and with that new-found determination, I went back to school."

This time, she graduated, then spent two years interning with a Seattle doctor. Then, with medical degree in hand, she decided to move back to Washington, D.C. With $30,000 worth of student loans to repay, Sullivan spent seven months working two jobs—serving as an executive assistant for a local council member by day, and seeing patients from seven to eleven o'clock at night. But it was a grueling schedule, so Sullivan decided that it was high time she hang out her own shingle. She gave her employers one month's notice and started promoting her practice by handing out flyers on the street and in local health food stores.

Today, Dr. Andrea Sullivan is one of the most respected naturopaths in the world. She is a founding member of the American Association of Naturopathic Physicians. She lectures nationwide, frequently appears on radio and television, and is the author of *A Path to Healing*. Her practice is also thriving—with a three-month waiting list. "I had the intention of saving the world," she says. "Do I do that? Maybe not, but I assist people in having a better quality of life, and that makes *my* life very rich and very full."

Lean on others. When Esther's world came crashing down, she didn't try to tough it out alone. The fact that she told Mordecai, "Go gather the Jews and fast for me" is a clear indication that she did not assume she was going to accomplish her mission single-handedly, notes Carol M. Bechtel, author of *Interpretation: A Bible*

Commentary for Teaching and Preaching. "Her reference to fasting acknowledges that she was relying on others—and perhaps God, although the reference is oblique—for success."

Having strong relationships—people who will listen and offer help and encouragement—can cushion even the most jarring jolts in life. "Resilience is embedded in relationships," agrees Froma Walsh, Ph.D., professor of psychology at the University of Chicago, and author of *Strengthening Family Resilience.*

And that's good news for women, who, by nature, tend to confide in others rather than keep their feelings bottled up. Trouble is, when we feel most vulnerable, we often hesitate to turn to others for help. Our take on failure: "I don't want to talk about it."

Big mistake. One of the standout findings of resilience research is that people who cope best with adversity are the ones who reach out to others—family, friends, support groups—for help.

One 40-year landmark study, for example, found that even among children raised in poverty with dysfunctional, mentally ill, or alcoholic parents, the majority—amazingly—grew up to be happy, well-adjusted adults. Their saving grace? Most belonged to social organizations like church groups or 4-H, or they had positive role models—teachers, mentors, close friends, etc.—to support them.

Other research confirms this to be true. In his book *Against Terrible Odds: Lessons in Resilience from Our Children,* psychiatrist Saul Levine, M.D., talks of "the kid who grew up in the KKK and is now a church bishop . . . the 11-year-old gun runner who is now a gentle and successful father . . . the woman who lost everything in Auschwitz and is now a brilliant, caring psychologist. What I learned from these people is that everyone reaches out to someone. That's how they survive. That's what makes them resilient."

Think like an optimist. Practice looking on the bright side, even when it feels fake and corny, advises University of Miami professor of psychology Charles Carver, Ph.D. Sounds sappy, yes, but "acting the part of an optimist may create true optimism," he explains. "Each time you count on success and achieve it, your confidence will build."

In other words, success breeds success—a philosophy Carmen Bermudez swears by. "I arrived in the United States when I was 15 years old. I had never seen a telephone, a television, or heard English spoken," says the Costa Rican native whose father had abandoned her family when she was two, and who used to climb trees to pick fruit as a way to stave off hunger.

After moving to the United States, Bermudez cleaned houses with her mother to help make ends meet. It took her two years to save $54 to buy a typewriter so she could land a job as a secretary. After that, she worked as a flight attendant for TWA and was promoted to in-flight service manager. She then spent a decade helping to run her husband's investment firm before opening Mission Management & Trust Company in Tucson—the first minority—and woman-owned trust company in the country.

Bermudez always believed she would make something of herself. "As a child, I learned to outwit bulls, which were used on farms to keep livestock safe from mountain lions," she says. "And that gave me confidence to last a lifetime."

So did swimming with sharks in 1993, when she signed up for San Francisco's Escape from Alcatraz Triathlon, a notoriously difficult and dangerous event, as it involves swimming in frigid, shark-infested waters.

To train for this event—and to get used to cold water—Bermudez bathed in ice cubes every day for four months. "By the time I jumped into the 55-degree water off Alcatraz, I was ready," she recalls. "By the time I reached San Francisco, I was slightly overheated."

A year later, Bermudez launched her business, which manages investments for charities, wealthy individuals, and large companies. Her primary goal was to provide personalized service, something she felt her competitors did not offer.

From the get-go, however, Bermudez learned that being both female and Hispanic would be uniquely challenging. Arizona State regulators audited her three times in the first six months. And the Bank of America gave her less than 24 hours' notice before dropping her personal and business accounts—suspecting her, she believes, of money laundering.

"A large religious organization in Pennsylvania had wired $7 million to us in the first two weeks, and another $15 million was on the way, which made a lot of folks suspicious," she explains. "I obliged them with the name of my client, but the bank dropped me anyway."

Word of this injustice spread quickly through Tucson's tight-knit business community, and by the next morning, Bermudez had a new bank. "The rest is history," she says gleefully. "We've been recognized nationally and internationally, and that bank no longer exists!"

Adjust your explanatory style. Here's another benefit to thinking like an optimist. Folks with a half-empty viewpoint tend to assume blame for all their failures, says Susan G. Vaughn, M.D., author of *Half-Empty, Half-Full: Understanding Psychological Roots of Optimism*. "Every mistake provokes anxiety. Any success seems like a fluke." On the flip side, people with a half-full per-

ROYAL ADVICE

I work for a large public relations firm, where I'm in charge of publications. I recently delegated final proofreading of a client's brochure to my assistant; now I've learned that it contained a major error. My boss is going to hit the roof, and I will probably be reprimanded since I delegated a job that was my ultimate responsibility. Should I reprimand my assistant? Should I tell my boss what happened—or hope, by some miracle, that he never finds out about it?

When you fail at something, it's important to fess up. Don't get defensive, and don't try to blame others. Be accountable. As painful as it may be, it's the only way to earn the respect of others and improve your chances of career success.

How so? When researchers at the Center for Creative Leadership compared the careers of twenty successful executives to those of twenty who had derailed from the same companies, both types had made mistakes. But while the successful managers faced their errors head on—by notifying superiors of the situation, attempting to solve the problems they'd caused, learning from their mistakes, and then moving on—those who had derailed typically tried to deny or cover up their mistakes or pointed the finger at others.

spective tend to attribute difficulties not to personal shortcomings, but to transient conditions—a computer glitch, a boss in a bad mood—and having an off day.

What's more, because optimists usually expect the best outcome, they're more motivated to bring it about, adds Martin

Seligman, Ph.D., author of *Learned Optimism.* "And this means they are good problem-solvers, able to mount effective strategies for dealing with little—and not-so-little—difficulties."

Cultivate positive emotions. When facing failure or crises, we all become momentarily helpless, says Seligman. "The psychological wind is knocked out of us. We feel sad, the future looks dismal, and putting out any effort seems over-whelmingly difficult." But the ability to perceive bad times as temporary—and allowing yourself to experience positive emotions—is key to bouncing back.

University of Michigan psychologist Barbara Frederickson, Ph.D., discovered this to be true when she had a group of students fill out questionnaires that measured their resiliency, optimism, and satisfaction with life. While analyzing her data, the tragedy of September 11, 2001 occurred, giving her an unexpected but potentially illuminating variable to look at. So, she went back and gave the same students another questionnaire to assess the emotions they had experienced since 9/11.

To no one's surprise, the study found that the higher the students scored on the resilience test, the easier they bounced back from the tragic events of that dark day in history. But one finding made Frederickson take note: The test also revealed that the single thing that made the most difference between those who bounced back and those who did not was their ability to experience positive emotions in the wake of the crisis.

How this works: "Optimists think more creatively and efficiently and are more open to new information and new ways of doing things" Frederickson explains. "This different and broader way of thinking causes them to build a reservoir of social, intellectual, and physical strengths that gives them the ability to bounce back."

What's more, the effect is cumulative. Which means that the more positive emotions you experience, the more resilient you become, she adds. "It's an upward spiral that builds strength."

Find a way to make a crisis meaningful. Memorize this equation: Crisis X = Opportunity. Then recognize that it's altogether possible to make a crisis work to your advantage.

That's what Terri Bowersock, founder and owner of the Mesa, Arizona, Terri's Consign and Design Furnishing, Inc., did. As a child, Bowersock struggled in school. "While other second-graders were reading, I was staring at the alphabet trying to figure out what the letters meant," she recalls. "In third grade, my parents took me to a specialist for testing, and I was diagnosed with dyslexia, a learning disability that makes letters seem to 'jump around.'"

Bowersock created her business straight out of high school. "Any position requiring strong reading and writing skills was out of the question," she reports. "My reading ability was still at the third-grade level. In fact, I was incapable of filling out a job application."

But Bowersock was determined to succeed. "Sometimes our disabilities give us our drive," she believes.

Bowersock got the idea for her business on a trip to visit her father in Kansas City. There, she met some ladies who ran a consignment store for knick-knacks and small furniture. "I got so excited! I just knew I could do the same thing with bigger furniture like dining room sets, couches, and beds. That night, I created my version of a business plan. Instead of writing the plan, I drew it with crayons and colored pencils. Then I borrowed $2,000 from my grandmother and opened my first consignment furniture store with my childhood bedroom set and my mother's living room furniture as inventory."

In no time, Bowersock had repaid her grandmother. Since then, she has franchised her opportunity, has sixteen stores nationwide, and has built Terri's into a $25 million empire without any loans. She is also a sought-after motivational speaker, has received numerous awards in recognition of her achievements, and has even written a book, *Success: It Can Be Yours!*

"I never let the possibility of failure stop me," she says of her phenomenal success. "I also use the power of positive thinking. I write down all my negative thoughts and fears—then I burn them, bury the ashes, and let positive thoughts take their place."

Understand just how small the difference between success and failure really is. "It is human nature to perceive the gap between success and failure as gigantic," says Maxwell. "After all, when we fail, we often think that we are miles from success—just as we believe that when we succeed, we are miles from failure. But the reality is that the gap between the two is seldom very wide."

Case in point: "A batter who hits .320 might make $5 million a year, while one who hits .220 might only get $500,000," Maxwell explains. "All the .220 hitter must do to increase his salary tenfold is get one more hit for each ten times at bat. So, the lesson here is that to turn things around, all you have to do is *slightly* increase your ratio of successes to failures."

Keep your eye on the goal. To say that WNBA superstar Cynthia Cooper rose from humble beginnings and overcame astounding odds would be an understatement. Born and raised by a single mom in a drug- and gang-infested Watts section of Los Angeles, this middle child of eight siblings was beaten by her father and an older brother and molested by a stranger. Years later, another of Cooper's brothers was stabbed to death, and more recently—in the space of six months—she lost both her mother and her best friend and teammate, Kim Perrot, to cancer.

Through all of this, Cooper has managed to persevere, even shine. Amazingly, she didn't even start playing basketball until the age of sixteen. Nevertheless, she was good enough to go pro and led the Houston Comets to four consecutive WNBA championships. Personally, she also won four straight MVP Awards, two ESPY Awards, an Olympic Bronze Medal (1992) and Olympic Gold (1998).

Since retiring from the NWBA, Cooper has signed a recording contract with Virgin Records, written three books and founded the Mary Cobbs "Build a Dream" Foundation—in honor of her late mother—which helps raise funds for breast cancer research. She is also CEO of Cooper-Metoyer Communications, a company she cofounded with pal and business partner Lavaille Metoyer.

"The things I've gone through have built my character and strength," she writes in her memoirs, *She Got Game: My Personal Odyssey*. "I knew that to get out of Watts, I had to concentrate on my goals. Because I was able to stay focused on them then, I'm able to do the same now. I continue to surprise myself."

Keep pushing yourself. Never forget that without failure, there is no achievement, advises Maxwell. "As the saying goes, 'Defeat may serve as well as victory to share the soul and let the glory out.'" In other words, the only way you can *really* reach your potential is to push yourself to your outer limits, as Esther did. "Until you encounter that point where you've done your absolute best (even if your 'best' turns out not to be good enough), there's no way of knowing just how far you can go—and what skills you'll need to learn in order to go even farther next time."

HANDLE ADVERSITY LIKE A QUEEN

In terms of facing challenges and dealing with adversity, Esther emerges as the ultimate role model. She wasn't afraid to put herself in the line of fire or to fight for what she believed in. She had the courage and faith to do what she believed was right. And the legacy she left behind inspires the rest of us to do the same when we face rock-bottom moments.

Oprah Winfrey, one of the world's most recognized and respected women, believes that within all of us lies a queen waiting to claim her glory. Winfrey shared this poignant message in a commencement address to the graduates of all-female Spelman College:

> Be a queen. Dare to be different. Be a pioneer. Be a leader. Be the kind of woman who in the face of adversity will continue to embrace life and walk fearlessly toward the challenge. Take it on! Be a truth seeker and rule your domain, whatever it is—your home, your office, your family—with a loving heart.
>
> Be a queen. Be tender. Continue to give birth to new ideas and rejoice in your womanhood. My prayer is that we will stop wasting time being mundane and mediocre. . . . We are daughters of God—here to teach the world how to love . . .
>
> It doesn't matter what you've been through, where you come from, who your parents are—nor your social or economic status. None of that matters. What matters is how you choose to love, how you choose to express that love through your work, through your family, through what you have to give to the world . . .
>
> Be a queen. Own your power and your glory! ♛

9

LET THE STORY
BE TOLD

*T*he thirteenth day of the twelfth month of Adar arrived—the day the enemies of the Jews had hoped to conquer them. But the tables had turned. Now the Jews had the upper hand over those who hated them . . .

> The Jews gathered in their cities in all the provinces of King Ahasuerus to strike out at those who sought to harm them, and no one could stand against them, because fear of them had fallen upon all the peoples.
> —*Esther 9:2*

Suddenly, thanks to Esther, the Jews were no longer underdogs . . .

> Now all the princes of the provinces and the satraps and the governors and the king's executive officers were promoting the Jews, because fear of Mordecai had fallen upon them. For Mordecai was important in the palace and his reputation was spreading throughout all the provinces, since the man Mordecai was growing increasingly important. And the Jews slaughtered all their enemies by the sword, slaying and destroying, and so wreaked their will on their enemies.
> —*Esther 9:3–5*

Neither Esther's contribution to saving her people nor her story of courage will ever be forgotten. That's because this amazing tale of a young woman who rose from orphan girl to beauty queen to heroic savior was recorded by ancient scribes. And today, Jews the world over are commanded to read the Megillah (Esther's story) not just once, but twice each year to commemorate this historical event.

Pretty good PR for a beauty queen who lived 2,500 years ago!

Unfortunately, most of us today can't afford a scribe to chronicle our everyday success. Nor can we command others to publicly tell our story each year. Thus, if we want to be successful, the obligation becomes our own. And therein lies the problem for many capable women, who don't feel comfortable telling their stories and tooting their own horns. Let us introduce you to two . . .

First came the rumors, the low rumblings, and buzzing at the watercooler. Then came the memo. The Fortune 500 insurance company where Karen Baker had worked in middle management for six years was downsizing.

Baker's reaction? To lay low and bury herself in work, convinced that her superiors would notice her dedication.

"Big mistake," Baker says in retrospect. "I got laid off, but my colleagues who were more visible and called attention to their successes survived the cut. And many had far less seniority than I did."

Public relations specialist Diane Solomon makes a living marketing her clients' talents. But when called upon recently to showcase her own strengths, she dropped the ball.

"My boss nominated me for a prestigious professional award, which was quite flattering," she explains. But when the form called for a letter of recommendation from the nominator, Solomon's boss asked her to write the letter for his signature. "You'll do a better job of making yourself shine," he told her.

Ultimately, the award went to a far less accomplished woman in Solomon's field. "My boss claimed I didn't win because the letter I wrote was weak," she reports. "I'm just not good at selling myself."

These stories share a common thread: Both involve bright and ambitious women who didn't get the recognition and attention they deserved simply because they had a problem with self-promotion.

And they are far from alone. In a recent study of 322 male and female executives, behavioral scientist Shannon L. Goodson, coauthor of *The Psychology of Sales Call Reluctance: Earning What You're Worth in Sales*, found that women are considerably less comfortable promoting themselves than men. "Many believe that all self-promotion is unacceptable and have been taught that hard work alone is sufficient to put them eventually on par with men," she says. "They also tend to be 'over-preparers,' making sure their work is technically correct, but not assuring that it is noticed by influential people in the organization."

Truth is, it takes more than top-notch skills, good work, a glowing résumé, or tenure with a company to get ahead these days. No matter if you're a secretary or a scientist, an executive or an entrepreneur, if you want to be successful—if you want to advance faster and farther—you can't just mind your own business. You have to sing your own praises. You have to toot your own horn.

WHY WOMEN ARE OUT OF TUNE

Scores of working women have the brains, talent, and credentials to get ahead, but far too many find themselves passed over for that coveted job or promotion. Why? Because regardless of how capable a woman may be, if no one recognizes her achievements, she'll never get the credit or recognition she deserves. As P. T. Barnum once said, "Without promotion, something terrible happens . . . NOTHING!"

The problem is, since girlhood, many of us have been taught not to brag or boast. It's not polite. It's not ladylike. And it feels self-aggrandizing and immodest. So, little wonder that drawing attention to ourselves and our accomplishments goes against our grain.

Where does this leave us? Caught in a Catch-22—where ancient Persia meets the 21st century. For example:

- Our mothers taught us to be modest when complimented and to deflect praise by saying, "Oh, it was nothing." But what does the boss think when we refuse hard-earned accolades for a job well done?
- In school, we were taught not to blurt out, to raise our hands, and to wait patiently for our turn. But as women, how does that play out at a business meeting?
- As children, our parents preached to us over and over again, "Don't talk to strangers." But as career women, if we don't take the initiative to interact and network with

people we don't know, we aren't considered "players."
Plus, when it comes to job opportunities, we get left out
of the loop.

• Growing up, our elders told us that we must be twice as
good to go half as far (as men), but they also taught us to be
modest. "Don't get the big head." So are we too self-serving
in sending out a press release to tout our latest promotion?

In essence, tooting one's own horn doesn't come easily to
most women. Yet, if you're trying to land a job, get promoted,
launch a business, or increase sales, crowing is a must.

BRING ON THE TRUMPETS!

Lebanon, New Jersey, headhunter Nick A. Corcodilos, online host
and author of www.asktheheadhunter.com, shares this story of a
woman who knew how to crow.

Leslie was a successful manager at a very large retail chain.
Recently divorced, with two children to support, she decided she
needed a change of scenery and an opportunity to start over
somewhere else. "So I picked the city, identified the two best companies for me, and did lots of homework," she says.

One of the companies—an international clothing retailer—
invited Leslie for an interview. She knew she was one of many talented candidates in the running for this upper-level management
position, and on the plane, decided to change her attitude about
interviewing. "No more trying to sell myself based on my credentials. It wasn't enough," she told herself. "I had one goal: to
show them I could do the job."

As her interview hummed along, Leslie took a huge risk—
but one that made her credibility soar. "In the midst of explaining

exactly how I was going to make the company more successful, I got up and walked out the door," she says.

"Come on! No more talk! I'm going to show you what I can do," Leslie announced as she led her two interviewers onto the retail floor, where she started demonstrating changes that she would make to increase sales. By the time she was finished, the interviewers stood there speechless. Finally, one spoke up. "You're exactly what we're looking for," he told Leslie. "Someone who's ready to do the job. When can you start?"

When it comes to self-promotion, few of us are as gutsy and up-front as Leslie. Yet, it's sheer confidence and enthusiasm like hers that goes a long way in persuading higher-ups that you've got what it takes to make *them* look good and to motivate others.

So, what's holding *you* back from blowing your own horn? Chances are, those outdated cultural messages and social conditioning are mostly to blame. Growing up, so many of us were taught that it was unladylike to draw attention to ourselves—that it was egotistical and boastful.

Indeed, in her landmark five-year study, Harvard University professor Carol Gilligan, Ph.D., found that as girls enter adolescence, they begin to submerge their personalities under the cultural mask of femininity. "Girls are afraid to speak up for themselves because they see that women who do are often spoken about and ostracized," says Elizabeth DeBold, a member of the Harvard Project on Women's Psychology and Girls' Development, who worked on Gilligan's study.

Is it any surprise, then, that even when we do shine, so many of us feel vaguely apologetic about it? As Lois Wyse once noted, "Men are taught to apologize for their weaknesses, women for their strengths."

So, what do men know that we don't? That the key to success is visibility—even if it means turning the spotlight on yourself. Yet, what's mere *strategy* to men too often becomes an *issue of morality* for us. "Women still perceive the word *self* as being wrong or wicked," acknowledges Donna Coulson, a management consultant in Red Bank, New Jersey. "But self-promotion is not being egotistical or boastful. It's letting people know you're around."

Adds Judith Rutkin with the Washington, D.C.–based firm iCoach America, "Women often become confused when their good work is not recognized. And most likely it won't be—unless you point it out to others."

The good news is, promoting yourself doesn't have to make you cringe. "The goal," Rutkin adds, "is to come across in a positive light that establishes your credibility without appearing boastful or self-aggrandizing."

TACTICS THAT SAY "HIRE ME"

An interview setting is custom-made for telling your story. In fact, interviewers *expect* you to toot your own horn. After all, no one else knows how well you can do for a job as you do.

Still, women are reluctant to promote themselves because doing so just doesn't feel comfortable. But as Tory Johnson, CEO of Women for Hire, points out, "There's a very clear distinction between bragging or lying versus touting your professional accomplishments and showing potential employers how fabulous you are. The point is to highlight why you're the right person for the job. And while it may feel uncomfortable spelling out what makes you so wonderful, it's absolutely a necessary task if you want to land a job."

The thing is, there are likely hundreds—maybe even thousands—of people who do—or dream of doing—exactly what you do for a living. And that means you need to find a way to stand out from the crowd.

How to shine at an interview? These tried-and-true strategies rarely fail:

Make your résumé sparkle. "In all the seminars we conduct, downplaying one's success in a résumé rates as a chief problem," says Johnson. And she's not talking about presentation, formatting, or even properly listing your marketable skills and experience. "More often than not, I see great companies and great qualifications, but one of the major problems is not quantifying or qualifying successes, which is what a savvy recruiter is looking for."

In other words, most résumés don't spell out what you can bring to the job. "Nobody cares if you were an account executive at a Fortune 100 company. But they would care if you continuously exceeded your quotas or were recognized with sales honors and awards," Johnson says. "Nobody cares if you were a marketing director at a dot-com, but they would care if the marketing promotion you created and executed helped triple Web traffic. But how will they know all this if you don't tell them?"

Bring your "Hall of Fame" with you. Accomplished something recently that you're especially proud of? If so, Therese Droste of monster.com, an Internet job site, suggests putting it in a file and bringing it with you to your interview. "For example, your folder might contain an extremely difficult report you pulled together for your manager at the eleventh hour and any accolades you received for your work on the project." That way, when the interviewer asks, "Do you work well under pressure?" or "How do you handle tight deadlines?" you can play show-and-tell.

ROYAL ADVICE

I recently finished graduate school and accepted an entry-level management position with a large telecommunications company. There's plenty of opportunity to advance quickly in this company, so I want to make a great impression on my bosses right away. What are some strategies I can use to get noticed—and promoted?

Aside from doing outstanding work—which is a no-brainer—you need to figure out ways to bring attention to yourself. For example, put the bulk of your energy into projects that have measurable results. Higher-ups pay the most attention to those who find ways to boost the bottom line.

Another tried-and-true strategy: Volunteer to take on a difficult project. Do it well, and your boss will likely reward you.

Finally, pinpoint the jobs you aspire to and determine what skills and training you're lacking to fill those positions. Then, take classes, sign up for seminars, read journal articles, etc. on your own to get what you need to forge ahead. As you get extra training, be sure to send out press releases so that your accomplishments can be announced in the company newsletter and in the local press. This will increase your visibility among higher-ups and may even get your name on the short list when promotions arise.

Be ready to respond to "Do you have any questions about the job?" This is a classic question that almost every interviewer poses, and you can use it to promote yourself. How so? "By subtly referring to your skills in your questions about the job," Droste explains. Example: "What I have found most rewarding in my present job is building a team, developing its goals, and then working to accomplish those goals. Will I have the opportunity to do that in this position?"

SELF-PROMOTION POWERPLAYS

Diane Contrisciano is a poster child for self-promotion. She began her career as a secretary in the marketing department at Mellon Financial Corporation in Philadelphia. Soon she was one of two employees tapped to build the office's marketing and planning department from the ground up. "We learned by the seat of our pants," she recalls.

Since then, Contrisciano has climbed the ranks to assistant vice president of the company. She credits her success to the public relations campaign—starring herself—she waged over the years. "Whenever I received verbal accolades from clients within the bank, I asked them to put their comments in writing and send them to my manager," she says. "And if my supervisor congratulated me on a job well done, I'd copy my boss's manager at Mellon's headquarters in Pittsburgh. If you're going to get promoted, people have to know who you are, what you're doing."

There are plenty of ways to take charge of your success and make great things happen in your career. So what are you waiting for? Grab a megaphone and start crowing! Here's how:

Take credit for your accomplishments. Men will do this in a heartbeat—and for any success even *remotely* related to their work. On the flip side, women are often reluctant to take credit for their achievements and, instead, frequently attribute their success to others or to sheer luck. Why? Usually out of fear that self-pride will interfere with the development of on-the-job relationships. However, by denying yourself credit for a job well done, you not only discount your strengths, you also cheat yourself out of the opportunity to get the attention and recognition you deserve.

Create your personal "elevator speech." High-level executives say they don't often hear about women's accomplishments. Ellen Snee, president of Fine Line Consulting, a Newton, Massachusetts, firm dedicated to the advancement of female corporate leaders, has a hunch why this is. "Most of the women we work with are extremely effective leaders, but they're often not good at drawing attention to their achievements," she says. Her solution? "Women should not assume their peers and managers know about their accomplishments. They must make a conscious effort to name and claim the work they do."

To help you do this, Snee advises coming up with a self-promotion spiel you can use to flaunt your talents. "If you end up in the elevator with the vice president or CEO, do you talk about the weather, or do you talk about your recent successes?" she asks. "In the time it takes to go from the third floor to the fifth floor, you can gain recognition for your work."

Become a storyteller. Squeamish about trumpeting your talents? Another softer but still powerful way to promote your strengths is to use anecdotal stories that highlight your accomplishments, says Rutkin. "Have a 30-second brand statement ready that establishes who you are. By practicing this packaged self-promotion ahead of time, you will be prepared the next time you meet someone you want to impress."

Take a risk. What sets self-promoters apart from the rest of the pack? Their ability to spot—and seize—opportunities. Or, better yet, the ability to *create* situations in which they will stand out, even if doing so means risking rejection and humiliation.

Back when Anna Quindlen, a Pulitzer Prize–winning columnist for the *New York Times*, was competing for her first big-city newspaper job at the *New York Post*, she was determined to find a way to stand out from the other candidates. So, she went to her interview at the *Post* wearing a fedora with a press card in the brim. When the editor told her that the job had been narrowed to two finalists—Quindlen and a recent Harvard graduate—she went home and made up a mock extortion note to send as a follow-up. "I cut out letters from magazines and newspapers and pasted them on dirty brown paper," she recalls. The note said: "Hire Anna Quindlen or you sleep with the fishes." And it worked.

Speak up at strategy meetings. The whole point of self-promotion is to do as much as you can to increase your profile with decision-makers. "That way, they know who you are, what you do, and why you're there," says Linda Kammire Tiffan, managing director of the Atlanta office of HR Solutions, a search firm. When you speak up, you're seen as a valuable player. It's the ideal way to show that you are bright, can solve problems and have ideas.

Play the numbers game. Look for ways to measure the results of your work and keep records of what you do. Compare your results to past performance or the average performance of others in similar situations. If your results look good, send a report to your supervisor.

"In the past, people were promoted because they deserved it or because they had the potential to grow into the job," says Harry S. Chambers, president of Training Solutions, a training and consulting firm in Atlanta. "Those days are over. Today people are promoted because of what they can bring to the table. Do they have the ability to cut costs, increase productivity, impact a revenue stream, do things faster and cheaper?"

Revamp your business card. Your business card is a perfect medium for blowing your own horn. "Think of it as your one-minute marketing brochure," advises Raleigh Pinskey, author of *101 Ways to Promote Yourself.* "It has two sides, so use them." How? She suggests putting your face and your "message" (client comments, your company's mission, etc.) on the backside. "After all, the purpose of your business card is for others to remember you, be able to contact you easily, and to connect with you personally. And adding these touches can accomplish all of these goals."

Go high-tech. Register your first name-last name.com and put up a personal Web site that gives your credentials and promotes your accomplishments. It's also a great way to brag—without uttering a sound!

"Thank heavens for Web sites," says Susan RoAne, author of *How to Work a Room.* "They're the perfect place to weave our stories, do our bragging, and inform our clients and readers of all the news that is 'fit to print' about us. And nary a word has to come out of our mouths." RoAne's Web site has led to interviews on CNN and with *Cosmopolitan.* "My press kit is on the site to facilitate speaking engagements and there are even questions and tips for the media to help them interview me."

Take a seat on boards. Carol Deutsch, president of Communication Seminars in Asheville, North Carolina, has found a way to give back to her community *and* gain visibility at the same time. How? By sitting on several boards of directors—women who've done this to promote themselves say it can have a wonderful "domino effect."

Initially, it was Deutsch's organizational and fund-raising talents that led to an invitation for her to serve on the board of the local National Public Radio affiliate, WCQS. After leading a successful fund-raising drive for that organization, she was tapped to serve on the board of the Asheville Area Chamber of Commerce. Taking the lead on several key projects there, Deutsch gained credibility among top members of the business community. "That, in turn, led to an appointment to the board of the prestigious community foundation, which manages over $90 million of development funds for the region," she says.

Deutsch has used her board positions not only to contribute to the community, but to develop an outstanding reputation among Asheville's business leaders. Now you can bet whenever they need the aid of a communications consultant, Carol is the first one they call.

Meet the press. Get published or quoted in newspapers, magazines, and professional journals. Share your knowledge and know-how by writing a letter to the editor or by penning an op-ed piece.

Media are constantly looking for new stories and information that will interest their readers. Likewise, local talk radio stations and programs are always in need of interesting guests. So, watch for times when your area of expertise fits with a breaking story or issues the media are covering.

Taking these steps will establish your credibility and solidify your authority. It will also get your name out there, and in no time, people who matter will be buzzing about you.

Putting in plenty of face time at networking events. Sitting on the sidelines will never get you noticed—or enable you to "tell your story." You have to get out there and schmooze. As

ROYAL ADVICE

My boss recently praised me profusely at a meeting after I gave a presentation on a project I'd been working on for months. After the meeting, several colleagues also complimented me on a job well done. All of that attention made me a bit uncomfortable, so I kept insisting, "I was just in the right place at the right time"—then I gave all the credit to my team. Now my mentor is on my case because he says I don't know how to take credit for my achievements. What does he mean?

Your mentor is right. When you shrug off a compliment by using phrases like "It was nothing" or "It was luck"—or you transfer total credit to others—you devalue your achievements and risk being viewed as someone who doesn't believe in herself. Worse, by brushing aside a compliment, you imply that the person who praised you has made a mistake or has poor judgment. In essence, this kind of response diminishes the other person gift of words to you.

A better response? Smile and graciously and say "thank you." You know you deserved the recognition, so soak up the praise and bask in the glory!

a successful chemist points out in *Women Breaking Through* by Deborah J. Swiss, "Perceptions of how hard you work and perceptions about your accomplishments are probably, in many ways, as important as what you actually do. If you are quiet and, therefore, invisible, you won't be identified as someone who is competent. You won't be perceived as being particularly successful or having good ideas—which may not be valid, but it comes out that way."

Networking is the perfect outlet for self-promotion. As Peter Vogt, president of Career Planning Resources in Eden Prairie, Minnesota, points out, networking events are the ideal setting "to let people know of your interests, so they'll have their radar up for you."

Susan Varlamoff, program coordinator at the University of Georgia's Office of Environmental Sciences, agrees. She recently met April Dents, of the Ford Motor Company, at a legislative reception, and the two have not only kept in touch, they recently sealed a significant—and mutually beneficial—deal.

"After a short exchange, we realized that April's job—to test alternative fuel vehicles—fit well with my position to promote University of Georgia research in biofuels," says Varlamoff. "With a pledge to get together and 'do lunch,' we began an enviable collaboration."

Over the next six months, Varlamoff and Dents continued to communicate and explore ways they could work together. "We realized this could be a marriage made in environmental heaven," Varlamoff says.

Ultimately, Ford Motor Company selected the University of Georgia as the site to test alternative fuel vehicles. "The first vehicle to arrive on campus was a silver compressed natural gas F-150 truck belonging to none other than Ford CEO Bill Ford," Varlamoff reports.

Their partnership has continued to blossom. "The University of Georgia is now one of only two universities in the United

States testing Ford alternative fuel vehicles," Varlamoff says. "Our sisterhood holds great promise in finding economically viable ways to produce cleaner cars made from renewable sources."

Did Varlamoff and Dents click because they were both women working in male-dominated fields? Does gender matter when it comes to networking? Esther had her group of maidens to schmooze with. And many women say they prefer it that way. When networking in mixed company, they sometimes feel overwhelmed—even ignored.

Astrid Pregel, the first female Canadian consul general to be posted in Atlanta, Georgia, can relate "Most of my speaking engagements are over lunch or dinner that include a networking event," she says. "I usually just join the fray after checking in with the organizers. Of course, often the organizers will take me around and introduce me. But the real fun occurs when they don't."

How so? First, with a name like Astrid, many people aren't sure if Pregel will be a male or female, and expectations are generally that she will be a male. Plus, at five feet, five inches, Pregel often finds herself shorter than most males who are networking. As a result, "I have to work hard to join ongoing conversations that are a foot above my head," she laughs.

Pregel always introduces herself clearly, but finds that listening skills at networking events are not always top-notch. As a result, people often don't realize she's the consul general. "You should see the faces later when I am introduced to get up to speak. In fact, there are usually a number of people (mostly men), who come up to me afterwards to offer a card, which they didn't offer during networking. And they are typically a bit sheepish—which I truly appreciate. Hopefully, it will be harder for them to make this kind of mistake again."

A few years ago, Pregel hosted the international all-female Conference on Women Entrepreneurs at the Canadian Embassy in Washington. "At the end of the day, I realized that for the first time in my career, I had been networking and not a single person ignored me thinking I was a spouse or an assistant to a meeting participant!"

It's true that networking groups dominated by men can be overtly competitive and even exclusionary. At women-only events, however, the emphasis is typically on cultivating relationships and sharing information in a safe, noncompetitive environment.

When it comes to self-promotion, though, you need to schmooze with and tell your story to men as well as women, says Krys Doerfler, a former executive with ABC News International. "If you want to get ahead, you need to be an equal opportunity networker."

Expose yourself. Get involved at professional conferences within your industry. Serve as an officer or volunteer to chair a committee for a high-profile trade association or local civic group. Join a speakers bureau as a way of sharing—and flaunting—your knowledge while gaining exposure. Be willing to conduct seminars or workshops on behalf of your employer. Volunteer to be a guest speaker at schools and industry events. Participate in panel discussions at public forums.

In other words, leave no self-marketing stone unturned. And make no bones about it—these measures *will* get you noticed and will very likely enhance your net worth. ♛

10

CELEBRATING YOUR
OWN PERSONAL PURIM

*T*he Jews defended themselves with gusto and pride, and
precious few were lost. In honor of their salvation, Mordecai
wrote down all that had happened and issued a decree
that all Jews of Persia celebrate a holiday to commemorate their
deliverance.

> Mordecai recorded these events; he sent letters to all the
> Jews throughout the provinces of King Ahasuerus, near
> and far, to have them celebrate annually the fourteenth
> and fifteenth days of the month of Adar as the time
> when the Jews got relief from their enemies, and as the
> month when their sorrow turned into joy and their
> mourning into a day of celebration. He wrote them to
> observe the days as days of feasting and joy and giving
> presents of food to one another and gifts to the poor.
> —*Esther 9:20–22*

*He named the holiday Purim—after the lots that Haman
threw to decide which day to kill the Jews—and declared that it be
a holiday of joyful thanksgiving forever . . .*

> These days should be remembered and observed in
> every generation by every family and every province
> and in every city. And these days of Purim should never

> cease to be celebrated by the Jews nor should the
> memory of them die out among their descendants.
> —*Esther 9:28*

Today, Purim remains the most joyful Jewish holiday of the year. A Mardi Gras–like atmosphere prevails, and celebrations include feasting, drinking, and great merry-making.

Little girls dress up like Queen Esther and march in parades. And as the Megillah is read, everyone shouts and stomps to drown out the name of Haman whenever it is mentioned. Finally, we are instructed to drink liberally until we do not know the difference between the phrases, "Blessed is Mordecai" and "Cursed is Haman."

As with most Jewish holidays, feasting is also an important part of Purim. Everyone's favorite course? Dessert, of course, when hamantashen is served—a delicious triangular pastry filled with fruit and modeled after the shape of Haman's three-cornered hat.

In essence, the whole point of Purim was—and still is—for Jews to take pride in their successes and to celebrate their survival.

Today, women need to do the same. Unfortunately, in the all-work-and-no-play society we live in, most of us don't do nearly enough celebrating—and we suffer because of it.

How so? Studies show that celebrating life's victories offers a slew of benefits. It creates an air of success around you that attracts joy and gives value to your work. It also energizes and motivates you, giving you the confidence boost you need to succeed even more.

So, go ahead—declare a personal holiday in your honor now and then. Create your own royal rituals. And no matter how busy you are, always make time to celebrate professional milestones, personal successes—both large and small—and life's gifts in general.

Need some ideas to get you started? Try:

• Giving yourself the royal treatment. Quick! When was the last time you pampered yourself? Can't remember? Women, who are notorious for putting everyone else's needs and desires ahead of their own, rarely do this.

Yet, researchers say that indulging yourself occasionally can be extremely therapeutic. So, why not send yourself a big bouquet of flowers, or buy yourself something frivolous that you don't really need? Play hooky for a day—or at least an afternoon—and spend that time goofing off. Better yet, head for a spa and request the royal treatment. No guilt allowed—you know you've earned it!

Every year, Edie Fraser, president of the Business Women's Network, which represents over 30 million women worldwide, oversees the publication of a book titled *WOW! Facts*. It contains the latest statistics and data on the economic clout of women and minorities, and pulling it together is an enormous undertaking.

The book's most recent launch took place at the U.S. Senate, with female U.S. senators taking the lead in celebrating the economic advances of women. After a star-studded lunch in the senate dining room, Fraser decided to reward herself as well, with time off for personal celebration with her husband, Joe. The two flew to Europe and boarded a barge, where they spent ten days cruising down the Canal Midi in southern France.

• Marking milestones. How does an author honor a book—"my first child"—that still sells in bookstores after 13 years and has had a major revision released? If you're Susan RoAne, author of *How to Work a Room*, you throw a "Book Mitzvah."

ROYAL ADVICE

Who's got the time to celebrate? I'm serious about my career, but I want to have a life as well. In fact, I'm fed up with work taking precedence over quality family time and am seriously considering doing something about it. What are the ramifications of stepping down a rung on the ladder, making a lateral move to a position that offers flex time, or even refusing a promotion?

Your question is a familiar one. The once prevailing mindset that to succeed, our careers must take priority over the rest of our lives is quickly fading. Balance is today's buzzword—and to find it, scores of working women are cutting back, staying put, or stepping off the promotion path.

For most, this plateauing on purpose is a temporary move. And sometimes careers stall in the process. But studies show this, too, is typically temporary.

Meanwhile, the tradeoffs are tremendous. Women are discovering that it is balance, not power or prestige—and certainly not a fat paycheck—that enables us to truly enjoy our work, keeps our lives from spinning out of control, and provides us with the gift of time to celebrate life's milestones that matter most.

"Friends and family (*mishpucheh*) celebrated the joyous occasion at a catered champagne reception at Willie's Café in Kentfield, California," she recalls. "Book mitzvah decorations of blue Stars of David covered the poles, banisters, counters, and tables to enhance the theme. The original cover photo of *USA Today* from 1988 with me at a New York party served as a centerpiece. On the menu: chopped liver flown in from New York and served on toasted challah squares. And for dessert: a traditional cake—in the shape of a book, of course—with the original cover as the decoration."

A friend of RoAne's, Ruthie Hirsch, sang a version of "Matchmaker, Matchmaker," "which we collaborated on and changed the words to 'Networker, Networker, make me a match,'" RoAne laughs. "And my proud mom stood on the sidelines and kvelled."

• Noshing some "hamantashen." Those long hours you and your staff have been logging lately have finally paid off: Quarterly sales are up! To celebrate, how about sharing a glass or two of wine with your team? Or, better yet, order a custom-made cake and pop open a bottle of champagne. You have every reason to celebrate!

• Paying homage to your supporters. RoAne's "Book Mitzvah" included the traditional candle-lighting ceremony—"honoring family and friends who supported me through thick and thin and who helped make my book a success," she says. "That first candle was, for course for Mumsy. Anyone who knows me for longer than two minutes knows that she is my anchor, my advisor, my rock."

But celebrations need not involve a lot of pomp and circumstance. They can be as quiet and low-key as creating a gratitude ritual. So, whenever you reach a goal, take time to give thanks for all the help you received, both human and divine.

And don't forget the "little people" who helped you shine. Recently *Time* magazine named Evelyn Hannon one of last century's "100 Most Innovative Thinkers." Hannon was tapped for creating Journeywoman.com, "an online travel resource for women—females helping females to travel safely and well. That success and recognition was a truly sweet reward at the end of a big and bumpy road," she says.

Hannon says she celebrated that success openly. "After all, I earned it!" But she felt especially grateful to her team of supporters worldwide. "I never ever lose sight of the fact that I didn't get where I am today without the help of all those women who assisted and encouraged me in endless different ways," she says. "I take every opportunity to say thank you to those in my community. Any awards that I receive are always accepted in the name of every one of those sisters instrumental in creating our international network of women who help each other to travel safely and well. I could never had done it without them—and I think they understand that."

• Drowning out your detractors. When you succeed at something, most people will applaud you. But there will typically be one or two who are jealous and resentful. Don't let the naysayers burst your bubble. Blanche Lambert Lincoln didn't. When she was elected to Congress at the age of 33, she recalls that some of the older congressmen just couldn't get over it. "Why, I have granddaughters who are your age!" one of them exclaimed. Lincoln flashed a big smile and replied, "I bet your granddaughters are glad I'm here." Five years later, no doubt those congressmen were even more stunned when Lincoln became the youngest woman ever elected to the Senate.

And when it came to achieving success as a newscaster, Barbara Walters definitely had her share of critics. "I did have a funny Boston accent, I couldn't pronounce my R's, and I wasn't a beauty," she acknowledges. And she was once told, "You're a marvelous girl, but stay out of television," by Don Hewitt—now the executive producer of *60 Minutes*!

In the 1970s, even before she went on the air to coanchor *ABC News*, the press called Walters, by then a 13-year veteran of NBC's *Today* show, "an overpaid prima donna," and reviews were dreadful. But Walters ignored these critics, focusing instead on kind words from her supporters—like John Wayne.

She had never even met the star, but he sent her a telegram. "The wire said, 'Don't let the bastards get you down,'" she reports. "And reading it, I felt as if the cavalry was coming. John Wayne's words taught me that you can't live your life around what other people may say about you. You've got to keep your chin up."

• Heralding all of your accomplishments—large and small. When Marilyn Carlson Nelson took over the multibillion-dollar travel conglomerate Carlson Companies—sweet justice after years of trying to convince her father that a woman could run the family business—she celebrated by flying in an F-16 fighter jet with the Air Force Thunderbirds, pulling nine g's over the Nevada desert.

But who says you have to wait until you finish an entire project to celebrate? Set short-term goals and reward yourself when you complete them.

• Performing a mitzvah (a good deed). In Esther's day, Purim was celebrated by giving to the poor. Acknowledging your good fortune by sharing with others less fortunate remains a wonderful way to celebrate. For example, you might make a donation to your favorite charity, send a check to your synagogue, or add a little extra to the collection plate at your church. You could give of your time as well—by signing up to serve at a soup kitchen, for instance.

Cynthia Kersey started her career as a secretary and rose to the top of her field as a sales executive, earning a six-figure income, for Sprint. To celebrate her success, she decided to quit her job, cash in her life's savings and do something "more fulfilling." As a result, she spent 18 months interviewing hundreds of America's greatest achievers.

Today, Kersey is a national columnist and the proud author of the best-selling book *Unstoppable: 45 Powerful Stories of Perseverance and Triumph from People Just Like You*. She is also an active volunteer for Habitat for Humanity and is spearheading projects to build 200 homes in Nepal and 100 homes in Guatemala.

A mitzvah can also entail doing something wonderful for someone else. When Oprah Winfrey's mentor and supporter, Maya Angelou, turned 70, for example, the talk show host honored her in a big way. "I planned a birthday party for her, asking her to invite 70 of her closest friends to a week-long party aboard the *Seabourn Pride*. The cruise was to the 'Mayan' ruins in Tulum, Mexico," Winfrey writes in *O* magazine.

Since the voyage occurred over Easter, guests awoke that Sunday morning to find fuzzy bunny slippers to wear to a sunrise service on deck. The afternoon included grown-up Easter egg hunts, a bunny hop, and a full-blown shipboard Easter parade.

"It was a wild week, made even more fun because most of the people there had known Maya her entire life," says Winfrey. "And for the guests—educators, authors, businesspeople, artists—this was a chance to let go of everyday restraints and responsibilities and just play. It was the most fun I've ever had watching so many other people have a blast."

• Parading your accomplishments. Surely you've heard of the "Sweet Potato Queens." This hilarious phenomenon started in 1982, when Jill Conner Browne and a group of her friends decided that every woman is endowed with queenliness. So, they donned Goodwill formals, placed tiaras on their heads, and marched in the Jackson, Mississippi, St. Paddy's parade.

That tradition continues, and each year the queens' outfits get more outrageous. Moreover, the queens' following of adoring fans has skyrocketed.

In 1999, Browne wrote down the queens' philosophies in *The Sweet Potato Queens Book of Love*, which has sprouted Sweet Potato Queen clubs nationwide (1,326 to date). This sisterhood, comprised of self-proclaimed royals, is devoted to getting together on a regular basis and celebrating regally. "All of us need an excuse to celebrate," believes Browne. "We just love to play, and that's the chord all of this has struck with people."

So if you feel like celebrating by making a lot of noise, you may want to become a Sweet Potato Queen yourself. To join the fun—and find a group near you—log on to www.sweetpotato queens.com.

Of course, if this sounds a bit too *meshuggeneh* for you, another more subtle way to parade your accomplishments is to send out press releases announcing your successes. Strategies like this also command attention—plus get you the regal recognition you deserve!

So, grab the tiara . . . sound the trumpets . . . break out the crown jewels . . . summon the maids-in-waiting. It's time to proclaim yourself Queen for a Day! You've earned it . . . you deserve it . . . give yourself the right to claim it.

And may you reign supreme! ♚

AFTERWORD

An Ancient Archetype for Women Today

Esther's story is "not about ancient Persia—it's about us!" believes Charles Swindoll, author of *Esther: A Woman of Strength and Dignity*. Indeed, this centuries-old saga is very much a story of modern times, filled with lessons that are timeless and universal.

Here was a woman who, against all odds, rose to the top of her profession. And after reading her story, there's no question about how she did it.

Esther knew how to use her grace and charm to impress and persuade others. She understood the importance of corporate culture and could play office politics with the best of them. She knew when to turn to others for advice and guidance and when to make decisions on her own. She was a powerful communicator and a savvy strategist who knew when to be bold and when to back off.

Above all, Esther's story is an inspiration. Throughout her life, she faced grave dangers and formidable challenges. Yet, despite these obstacles, she managed to keep the faith and persevere.

Given all that Esther knew, it's little wonder that her story continues to inspire women—even after 2,500 years. And what makes her story so uplifting? Unlike many other biblical figures, Esther was not perfect; she was human. And as Michael V. Fox points out in *Character and Ideology in the Book of Esther*, "Her very ordinariness suggests that ordinary people, too, can rise to the moment and take on unexpected strengths." Moreover, Esther's power and leadership were not divinely imposed, they were earned as "the result of a difficult process of inner development and self-realization."

Finally, the story of Esther is not about miracles, but about a courageous woman who used her intellectual and spiritual resources to overcome adversity and ultimately to triumph. ☙

REFERENCES

Introduction

Bechtel, C. *Interpretation: A Bible Commentary for Teaching and Preaching.* Louisville, KY: John Knox Press, 2002.

Booher, D. *The Esther Effect: The Seven Secrets of Confidence and Influence.* Nashville, TN: W. Publishing Group, 2001.

Dole, E. "Crisis and Faith." In: K. Monroe (ed.) *Finding God at Harvard.* Grand Rapids, MI: Zondervan Publishing House, 1996.

Fox, M. V. *Character and Ideology in the Book of Esther.* Grand Rapids, MI: Wm. B. Eerdman's Publishing Co., 2001.

Swindoll, C. R. *Esther: A Woman of Strength and Dignity.* Nashville, TN: Word Publishing, Inc., 1997.

Chapter 1

Ascending to Power: Making a Royal First Impression

Alessandra, T. *Charisma: Seven Keys to Developing the Magnetism That Leads to Success.* New York: Warner Books, 1998.

Anderson, K. "Creating a Positive First Impression." *Nursing* (March 1998).

Benton, D. A. *Lions Don't Need to Roar: Using the Leadership Power of Professional Presence to Stand Out, Fit In, and Move Ahead.* New York: Warner Books, 1992.

Bixler, S., and L. S. Dugan. *5 Steps to Professional Presence: How to Project Confidence, Competence, and Credibility at Work*. Holbrook, MA: Adams Media Corporation, 2001.

Breen, B. "Interview with a Headhunter." *Fast Company* (January 1999): p. 154. www.fastcompany.com/online/21/toolbox.html.

Brenner, R. C. *Body Language in Business: How to Sell Using Your Body*. San Diego, CA: Brenner Books, 1998.

Brooker, K. "It Took a Lady to Save Avon." *Fortune* (October 15, 2001): p. 203.

Buhler, P. "What Is Corporate Culture and Why Is It Important?" *Supervision* (September 1993): p. 17.

Caputo, T. A. "Get Hired for Your Dream Job." *Woman's World* (June 26, 2001): p. 44.

Conlin, M. "She's Gotta Have 'It.'" *Business Week* (July 22, 2002): p. 85.

Corcodilos, N. A. *Ask the Headhunter: Reinventing the Interview to Win the Job*. New York: Plume, 1997.

Corcodilos, N. A. "Women and Interviews: Brassy, Foolish Dames." www.asktheheadhunter.com/women8.htm.

Field, A. "Coach, Help Me Out with This Interview." *Business Week* (October 22, 2001): p. 134 E2.

Glaser, C. B., and B. S. Smalley. *More Power to You: How Women Can Communicate Their Way to Success*. New York: Warner Books, 1992.

Glaser, C., and B. S. Smalley. *Swim with the Dolphins: How Women Can Succeed in Corporate America on Their Own Terms*. New York: Warner Books, 1995.

Greco, S. "Finding the Perfect Pitch." *Inc.* (June 2002): p. 88.

Jobes, K. H. *Esther: The NIV Application Commentary.* Grand Rapids, MI: Zondervan Publishing House, 1999.

Navarro, A. "Dressing Suitably for the Workplace Is a Uniform Rule." *St. Louis Business Journal* (March 19, 1999): www.bizjournals.com/stlouis/stories/1999/03/22/smallb5.html.

Sharpe, A. "As Leaders, Women Rule." *Business Week* (November 20, 2000): p. 74.

Siegel, M. "The Perils of Culture Conflict." *Fortune* (November 9, 1998): p. 257.

Slania, J. T. "The Search for a Financing Grail: One Entrepreneur's Funding Saga. *Crain's Online* (July 9, 2001): p. 3.

Solovic, S. W. *The Girls' Guide to Power and Success.* New York: AMACOM, 2001.

Swindoll, C. R. *Esther: A Woman of Strength and Dignity.* Nashville, TN: Word Publishing, Inc., 1997.

Voros, S. "Presence Counts for Women Candidates." www.careerjournal.com/salaries/industries/seniorexecs/20000801-voros.html.

Voros, S. "What Happens after the Interview; Financial Executives in Interviews." *Financial Executive* (January 11, 1997): p. 24.

CHAPTER 2

Find a Mentor to Open Your Eyes and Doors

Bramford, J. "Learning through Immersion." *Bloomberg Personal Finance* (June 1998). www.bloomberg.com/personal/archives/ftA9806-child.html.

Bechtel, C. *Interpretation: A Bible Commentary for Teaching and Preaching*. Louisville, KY: John Knox Press, 2002.

Brounstein, M. *Coaching and Mentoring for Dummies*. New York: John Wiley and Sons, 2000.

Church, E. "Mentors Guide Women Through Career Roadblocks." *Workopolis* (March 8, 2001). www.workopolis.com/servlet/News/fasttrack/20010308/MGWOME.

Corcodilos, N. "Mentoring and Getting Mentored." www.asktheheadhunter.com/hamentor.htm.

Crab, C. "Cracking Glass Ceilings: Right Mentor May Be Career Fix You Need." *The Hartford Courant* (April 9, 2001): p. E1.

Dahle, C. "Women's Ways of Mentoring. *FastCompany* (September 1998). www.fastcompany.com/online/17/womentoring/html.

Dalton, J. C. "More Room at the Top." *CFO, The Magazine for Senior Financial Executives* (August 1998): p. 30.

Dole, E. "Crisis and Faith." In: K. Monroe (ed.) *Finding God at Harvard*. Grand Rapids, Michigan: Zondervan Publishing House, 1996.

Einhart, N. "Survival Tactic: Recognize Your Female Talent." *Fast Company* (January 2001). www.fastcompany.com/lead/lead_feature/act_fineline.html.

"Executive Sweet." http://goldsea.com/WW/Jungandrea/jungandrea.html.

Fisher, A. "Women Need At Least One Mentor and One Pant Suit." *Fortune* (October 12, 1998): p. 208.

Gordon, A. *A Touch of Wonder*. New York: The Berkley Group, 1991.

Greengard, S. "Moving Forward with Reverse Mentoring." *Workforce* (March 2002): p.15.

Gutner, T. "In the Venture Drought, an Oasis." *Business Week* (July 16, 2001): p. 86 E2.

Gutner, T. "Three Simple Steps to the Top." *Business Week* (October 9, 2000): p. 2006 E8.

Hass, N. "Hey Dads, Thanks for the Love and Support (and the Credit Card). *New York Times* (June 16, 2002): sec. 9, p. 1.

Hennig, M., and A. Jardim. *The Managerial Woman*. New York: Doubleday and Company 1977.

Hobson, K. "Family Bonds." *Princeton Alumni Weekly* (February 27, 2002). www.princeton.edu/~paw/ archive_new/PAW01-02/10-0227/features2.html.

Isaacs, N. "Mentors Gain Ground: Formal and Informal Programs Point Workers in Right Direction. *InfoWorld* (October 5, 1998): p. 113.

Jwanier, D. "Women May Be Better Role Models, But Men Are Vital to Career Growth. *Penn State Intercom* (February 3, 2000): p. 15.

Jeruchim, J., and P. Shapiro. *Women, Mentors, and Success*. New York: Ballantine Books, 1992.

Jobes, K. H. *Esther: The NIV Application Commentary*. Grand Rapids, MI: Zondervan Publishing House, 1999.

Khirallah, D. R. "Set Goals and Meet Objectives the Mentoring Way." InformationWeek.com (June 3, 2002): p. 76.

Leaders' Edge Research. www.the-leaders-edge.com/ our_research/our_research_2000.html.

Lichtenberg, R. *It's Not Business, It's Personal*. New York: Hyperion, 2001.

Maaddi, R. "Study Says Women Mentors May Be Better Role Models, but Men Better Able to Advance Careers." The Associated Press (January 21, 2000).

"Mentoring, Alliancing Are Women's Answers to the 'Old Boys' Network.'" *About Women and Marketing Newsletter* (December 19, 1998).

Mieszkowski, K. "Radical Mentoring." *Fast Company* (September 1998): p. 104.

Moran, G. "The Mentor Advantage—How a Mentor Can Help Your Career or Business." www.bluesuitmom.com/career/management/mentoring.html.

Peddy, S. *The Art of Mentoring: Lead, Follow, and Get Out of the Way.* Corpus Christi, TX: Bullion Books, 2001.

Shaffer, B., Tallarica, B., and J. Walsh. "Win-Win Mentoring." *Nursing Management* (January 1, 2000): p. 32.

Simonetti, J. L. "Through the Top with Mentoring." *Business Horizons* (November 1999). www.findarticles.com/cf_0/m1038/6_42/58381521/print.jhtml.

"Sister Cities." *Fast Company.* www.fastcompany.com/lead/lead_feature/neuberger.html.

Steele, J. "Mentoring Offers Valuable Insights." *Chicago Tribune* (December 29, 1996): p. 52.

"The Hidden Pitfalls of Mentoring." *Businessweek Online* (April 17, 2001). www.businessweek.com/careers/content/apr2001/ca20010417_638.htm.

"The Many Faces of Mentoring." *American Management Association* (April 1997): p. C3.

Wellington, S., and B. Spence. *Be Your Own Mentor: Strategies from Top Women on the Secrets of Success.* New York: Random House, 2001.

CHAPTER 3

It Pays to Know the Palace Gossip

Allerton, H. E. "Myth Buster." *Training and Development* (March 2000): p. 96.

Browder, S. "Dishing in the Office." *New Woman* (May 1994): p. 74.

Dearlove, D. "I Heard It On the Grapevine." *The Times* (May 1, 1997): p. 1F3.

DeLuca, J. R. *Political Savvy: Systematic Approaches to Leadership Behind the Scenes.* Berwyn, PA: Evergreen Business Group, 1999.

Fisher, A. *If My Career's On the Fast Track, Where Do I Get a Road Map? Surviving and Thriving in the Real World of Work.* New York: HarperCollins, 2002.

Jaworski-Lang, H. "Danger: Friends at Work." *The Independent* (August 15, 1999): p. 11.

Jobes, K. H. *Esther: The NIV Application Commentary.* Grand Rapids, MI: Zondervan Publishing House, 1999.

Kennedy, M. M. *Powerbase: How to Build It/How to Keep It.* New York: Macmillan Publishing Company, 1987.

Keyishian, A. "How to Gossip to Get Ahead." *Cosmopolitan* (June 2000): p. 146.

Lichtenberg, R. *Work Would Be Great if It Weren't for the People: Ronna and Her Evil Twin's Guide to Making Office Politics Work for You*. New York: Hyperion, 1998.

Lloyd, K. *Jerks at Work*. Franklin Lakes, NJ: Career Press, 1999.

Mallory, M. "The Gaffe of Office Gab." *Atlanta Journal-Constitution* (May 5, 2002): p. R-1.

Nicholson, N. "The New Word on Gossip." *Psychology Today* (May/June 2001): p. 41.

RoAne, S. *The Secrets of Savvy Networking*. New York: Warner Books, 1993.

Swindoll, C. R. *Esther: A Woman of Strength and Dignity*. Nashville, TN: Word Publishing, Inc., 1997.

Warshaw, M. "They Hear It through the Grapevine." *Fast Company* (September 1998): p. 160.

Yager, J. *Friendshifts: The Power of Friendship and How It Shapes Our Lives*. Stamford, CT: Hannacroix Creek Books, 1999.

CHAPTER 4

Fighting for What You Believe In

Aushenker, M. "Challenging Evil." *The Jewish Journal of Greater Los Angeles* (June 30, 2000). www.freedomsite.org/pipermail/fs_discussion/2000-July/000528.html.

Bechtel, C. *Interpretation: A Bible Commentary for Teaching and Preaching*. Louisville, KY: John Knox Press, 2002.

Booher, D. *The Esther Effect: The Seven Secrets of Confidence and Influence*. Nashville, TN: W. Publishing Group, 2001.

Carlson, M. "A Woman of Substance." *Time* (July 30, 2001): p. 64.

Colvin, G. "Wonder Women of Whistleblowing." *Fortune* (August 12, 2002): p. 56.

"Critics Wonder: What About Enron?" *Atlanta Journal-Constitution* (July 31, 2002): p. D-1.

Davidson, R. "Full-Time Blown on the Old-Boys' Club." *The Sunday Tribune* (August 11, 2002): p. 2.

Duffy, M. "What Did They Know and When Did They Know It? *Time* (January 28, 2002): p. 16.

Farson, R., and R. Keyes. *Whoever Makes the Most Mistakes Wins: The Paradox of Innovation.* New York: The Free Press, 2002.

Fitzgerald, J. "Million-Dollar Question." *Chicago Tribune* (July 24, 2002): p. 1.

Fox, M. V. *Character and Ideology in the Book of Esther.* Grand Rapids, MI: Wm. B. Eerdman's Publishing Company, 2001.

Glaser, C., and B. S. Smalley. *Swim with the Dolphins: How Women Can Succeed in Corporate America on Their Own Terms.* New York: Warner Books, 1995.

Groves, M. "For Women, Taking Risks Is Key to Working Their Way Up the Ladder." *Los Angeles Times* (September 1, 1996): p. D-5.

Gutner, T. "Blowing Whistles—and Being Ignored." *Business Week* (March 18, 2002): p. 107.

Harden, C. "Auditor Who Blew the Whistle Praised." *Clarion-Ledger.com* (July 6, 2002): p. 1C.

Hundley, K. "Women Seize the Spotlight in Blowing Whistle on Fraud." *St. Petersburg Times* (July 13, 2002): p. 1E.

Hunt, A. R. "A Mighty Oak Falls in Washington." *The Wall Street Journal* (July 19, 2001): p. A23.

Jobes, K. H. *Esther: The NIV Application Commentary*. Grand Rapids, MI: Zondervan Publishing House, 1999.

Kelly, M. "Be the Mayor of Your Office." *Glamour* (March 2002): p. 123.

Lowenstein, R. "Kay Graham Deserved a Pulitzer for Management Too." *The Wall Street Journal* (July 23, 2001): p. A-14.

Pack, R. "Whistleblowers and the Law." *The Washington Lawyer* (June 2001): p. 20.

"Persistent Auditor Brought WorldCom Scandal to Light." *St. Petersburg Times Online Business* (July 13, 2002): p. 1E.

Pestrak, D. "Embracing Change and Taking Risks Can Enhance Your Career." *Success* (April 2001). www.debrapestrak.com/success_view_200104.htm.

Peters, H. "Risk, Rescue and Righteousness: How Women Prevent Themselves from Breaking through the Glass Ceiling." Hagberg Consulting Group. www.hcgnet.com/html/articles/female-executives.html.

Porretto, J. "WorldCom Outlines Discovery of Financial Scheme. The Associated Press (July 1, 2002).

Prussel, W. "Diane Creel, Earth Tech CEO." IMDiversity.com. www.imdiversity.com/villages/woman/Article_Detail.asp?Article_ID=1301.

Ratnesar, R., and M. Weiskopf. "How the FBI Blew the Case." *Time* (June 3, 2002): p. 24.

Reese, K. "Burden of Proof." *Emory Magazine* (Autumn 2000). www.emory. edu/EMORY-MAGAZINE/autumn2000/lipstadt.html.

Rosener, J. *Ways Women Lead*. Boston, MA: Harvard Business School Press, 2002.

Schooner, S. L. "Badge of Courage." *Government Executive Magazine* (August 1, 2002): p. 65

Scollard, J. *Risk to Win: A Woman's Guide to Success*. New York: Macmillan Publishing Company, 1989.

Smith, L. "Why Women Are the Fairer Sex." *The Hamilton Spectator* (July 8, 2002): p. C04.

Swindoll, C. R. *Esther: A Woman of Strength and Dignity*. Nashville, TN: Word Publishing, Inc., 1997.

Syrkin, M. *Golda Meir Speaks Out*. Pomfret, VT: Trafalgar Square, 1973.

Thomas, H. "Women Whistle-Blowers Did Right Thing." *The Houston Chronicle* (June 15, 2002): p. A-40.

Wellington, S., and B. Spence. *Be Your Own Mentor: Strategies from Top Women on the Secrets of Success*. New York: Random House, 2001.

"What Is It You Really Like to Do? BusinessWeek Online (July 19, 2001). www.businessweek.com/careers/content/jul2001/ca20010719_033.htm.

CHAPTER 5

Mapping Out Your Plan of Attack

Arditi, L. "To a Woman—Even with a Head Start, You Have to Take One Rung at a Time." *The Providence Journal-Bulletin* (March 14, 2002): p. E-01.

Arthur, J. S. "A Woman's Touch." *Human Resource Executive* (August 1999): p. 72.

Bechtel, C. *Interpretation: A Bible Commentary for Teaching and Preaching*. Louisville, KY: John Knox Press, 2002.

Booher, D. *The Esther Effect: The Seven Secrets of Confidence and Influence*. Nashville, TN: W. Publishing Group, 2001.

Cohen, E. "Mixing Manicures and Megabuck Deals." *People* (May 5, 1997): p. 89.

Dunham, K. J. "Getting Ahead. *The Wall Street Journal* (November 7, 2000): p. B-20.

Evans, G. *Play Like a Man, Win Like a Woman: What Men Know about Success That Women Need to Learn*. New York: Broadway Books, 2001.

Fisher, H. *The First Sex: The Natural Talents of Women and How They Are Changing the World*. New York: Ballantine Books, 2000.

Glaser, C., and B. S. Smalley. *Swim with the Dolphins: How Women Can Succeed in Corporate America on Their Own Terms*. New York: Warner Books, 1995.

Gutner, T. "Weaving an Old-Girls Network." *Business Week* (July 9, 2001): p. 115.

Harrari, O. *The Leadership Secrets of Colin Powell*. New York: McGraw Hill, 2002.

Jobes, K. H. *Esther: The NIV Application Commentary*. Grand Rapids, MI: Zondervan Publishing House, 1999.

Jones, L. B. *The Path: Creating Your Mission Statement for Work and Life*. New York: Hyperion, 1998.

Jones, L. B. *Jesus, CEO: Using Ancient Wisdom for Visionary Leadership*. New York: Hyperion, 1996.

Knouse, S. B. "Virtual Mentors: Mentoring on the Internet." *Journal of Employment Counseling* (December 1, 2001): p. 162.

Leary, B. "Brianne Leary's Gut Instincts." *O, The Oprah Magazine* (September 2002): p. 89.

Lichtenberg, R. *Work Would Be Great If It Weren't For the People: Ronna and Her Evil Twin's Guide to Making Office Politics Work for You.* New York: Hyperion, 1998.

Logue, A. C. "Girl Gangs." *Training and Development* (January 2001): p. 24.

Mallory, M. "Networking Not Just a Job Hunt." *Atlanta Journal-Constitution* (June 2, 2002): p. R-1.

Marks, M. A. "A Woman's Voice: Listening to Lipstadt." *The Jewish Journal of Greater Los Angeles* (May 5, 2000). www.jewishjournal.com/old/mam.5.5.0.htm.

Mills, H. *Artful Persuasion: How to Command Attention, Change Minds, and Influence People.* New York: AMACOM, 2000.

Paterson, J. "Career Connections." *Careers and Colleges* (January 2001): p. 35.

Robertson, I. *Mind Sculpture: Unlocking Your Brain's Untapped Potential.* New York: Fromm International, 2000.

Savacool, J. "Can You See Success From Here?" *Self* (December 2000): p. 101.

"Schmooze on Up: Office Socializing is a Good Thing." *Men's Health* (October 2001): p. 44.

Sellers, P. "Patient But Not Passive." *Fortune* (October 15, 2001): p. 188.

"Sister Cities." *Fast Company*. www.fastcompany.com/lead/lead_feature/neuberger.html.

Spence, B. "Not Separate, Not Equal." *Executive Female* (June/July 2001): p. 1.

Starcevich, M., and F. Friend. "Effective Mentoring Relationships from the Mentee's Perspective." *Business and Management Practices* (July 1999): p. 2.

Swindoll, C. R. *Esther: A Woman of Strength and Dignity*. Nashville, TN: Word Publishing, Inc., 1997.

Tannen, D. *Talking from 9 to 5: Women and Men in the Workplace: Language, Sex and Power*. New York: Quill, 2001.

"The World of Madeline Albright. *Newsweek* (February 10, 1997): p. 27.

"Who You Know Often a Key to Success for Small Business Owners: Small Business Exchange Web Site Helps Women Entepreneurs Sharpen Networking Skills. *Business Wire* (October 4, 1999).

CHAPTER 6

Communicating with the Clout of a Queen

Bechtel, C. *Interpretation: A Bible Commentary for Teaching and Preaching*. Louisville, KY: John Knox Press, 2002.

Booher, D. *The Esther Effect: The Seven Secrets of Confidence and Influence*. Nashville, TN: W. Publishing Group, 2001.

Bristow, W. "So Does Women's Intuition Exist?" *Daily Mail* (August 4, 1997): p. 44.

Fox, M. V. *Character and Ideology in the Book of Esther*. Grand Rapids, MI: Wm. B. Eerdman's Publishing Company, 2001.

Glaser, C. B., and B. S. Smalley. *More Power To You: How Women Can Communicate Their Way to Success*. New York: Warner Books, 1992.

Jobes, K. H. *Esther: The NIV Application Commentary*. Grand Rapids, MI: Zondervan Publishing House, 1999.

McIntosh, C. "Roll With the Hunches." *Essence* (June 2000): p. 109.

O'Brien, P. "Why Men Won't Listen." *Working Woman* (February 1993): p. 56.

Rose, J. "Follow the Money." *FSB* (March 2001): p. 72.

Swindoll, C. R. *Esther: A Woman of Strength and Dignity*. Nashville, TN: Word Publishing, Inc., 1997.

Tannen, D. *Talking from 9 to 5: Women and Men in the Workplace: Language, Sex, and Power*. New York: Quill, 2001.

Voros, S. *The Road to CEO: The World's Leading Executive Recruiters Identify the Traits You Need to Make It to the Top*. Avon, MA: Adams Media Corporation, 2000.

White, P. "Mixing Worlds." *Vive* (September/October 2001): p. 60.

CHAPTER 7

Dealing with Life's Hamans

Barnes, S. E. "Best Boss, Worst Boss." *Diversity Monthly* (February 28, 1999): p. 30.

Basinger, J. "Kennesaw State University Settles Religious Bias Law Suit with Former Instructor." *Chronicle of Higher Education* (March 20, 1998): p. A14.

Beier, S. "Workday Headaches: Don't Let Jealous Co-Workers Hold You Back." IMDiversity.Com. www.imdiversity.com/villages/woman/Article_Detail.asp?Article_ID=1266.

"Bosses: Can't Live with Them, Can't Eat without Them." *Ladies' Home Journal* (March 1994): p. 198.

Bramson, R. *Coping with Difficult Bosses*. New York: Fireside Publishing, 1994.

Caponigro, J. *The Crisis Counselor: A Step-by-Step Guide to Managing Business Crisis*. New York: McGraw Hill, 2000.

Ciabattari, J. "When Bad Bosses Happen to Good People." *Working Woman* (July 1989): p. 88.

"Corporate Cat Fighting: Do Working Women Keep Each Other Down at the Office?" *Good Morning America* (May 29, 2002).

Fabian, A. "Bully the Office Bully." *New Woman* (April 1998): p. 64.

Fox, M. V. *Character and Ideology in the Book of Esther*. Grand Rapids, MI: Wm. B. Eerdman's Publishing Company, 2001.

Gallagher, C. *Going to the Top: A Road Map for Success from America's Leading Women Executives*. New York: Penguin USA, 2001.

Goulet, T. "What to Do about Problem Supervisors." www.fabjob.com/articles3.htm.

Goulet, T. "Feedback Can Improve Bad Bosses." *The Ottawa Citizen* (December 20, 2000): p. E-5.

Hanson, C. "Mission Impossible? The Politics of Managing Friends. *Jugglezine* (May 3, 2002). www.jugglezine.com/CDA/juggle/0,1516,78,00.html.

Heffernan, M. "The Female CEO ca. 2002." *Fast Company* (August 2002): p. 58.

Heim, P., Murphy, S., and S. K. Golant. *In the Company of Women: Turning Workplace Conflicts into Powerful Alliances.* Los Angeles: J. P. Tarcher, 2001.

Jobes, K. H. *Esther: The NIV Application Commentary.* Grand Rapids, MI: Zondervan Publishing House, 1999.

Jones, T. "A Real Piece of Work: 'Worst Boss' Contest Lets Employees Vent." *The Washington Post* (October 16, 1997): p. B01.

Kelly, M. "Make Over Your Boss." *Glamour* (November 2001): p. 107.

Tannen, D. "Stand Up for Yourself at Work, at Home, in Life." *Good Housekeeping* (April 2001): p. 140.

Theim, R. "When Bad Bosses Happen to Good People: Misbehavior by Authority Is Tolerated in the Workplace—And Almost Nowhere Else." *Chicago Tribune* (December 16, 2001): p. 5.

Useem, M. *Leading Up: How to Lead Your Boss So You Both Win.* New York: Crown Publishing, 2001.

Weinstein, B. "My Boss Is a Lunatic!" *Milwaukee Journal-Sentinel* (May 15, 2002). www.jsonline.com/bym/Career/May02/43512.asp.

CHAPTER 8

Keeping the Faith

Aborn, S. "The Bounce Back Factor." *Ladies' Home Journal* (April 2001). www.findarticles.com/cf_0/m1127/4_118/72050043/print.jhtml.

Applegate, J. "These Entrepreneurs Would Not Be Deterred by Adversity." *Los Angeles Business Journal* (June 26, 2000): p. 24.

Barrett, G. "Last Survivor of World Trade Center Embraces New Life—And God." Gannett News Service (September 9, 2002).

Bechtel, C. *Interpretation: A Bible Commentary for Teaching and Preaching*. Louisville, KY: John Knox Press, 2002.

Blum, D. "Finding Strength: How to Overcome Anything." *Psychology Today* (May/June 1998): p. 32.

Booher, D. *The Esther Effect: The Seven Secrets of Confidence and Influence*. Nashville, TN: W. Publishing Group, 2001.

Bowersock, T. *Success: It Can Be Yours! How to Be a Millionnaire by Using Your Determination*. Phoenix, AZ: Terris Publishing and Speaking, 2000.

Cain, J. D. "The Art of Taking Risks." *Essence* (August 1999): p. 79.

Cain, J. D. "Buried Alive: Trapped Beneath Tons of Steel and Concrete Debris from the World Trade Center Collapse, She Prayed for a Miracle—And Got It." *Essence* (April 2002): p. 71.

Cloud, J. "A Miracle's Cost." *Time* (September 9, 2002): p. 33.

Cooper, C. *She Got Game: My Personal Odyssey*. New York: Warner Books, 2000.

Dunleavey, M. P. "Your Mission: To Fail." *Self* (June 2000): p. 134.

Forgrieve, J. "A Single Mom, Broke, She Fought Back." *The Tampa Tribune* (January 3, 2000): p. 5.

Fox, M. V. *Character and Ideology in the Book of Esther.* Grand Rapids, MI: Wm. B. Eerdman's Publishing Company, 2001.

Guida, T., and K. Pilgrim. "Schleppers Profile." *CNNfn* (August 22, 2000).

Jobes, K. H. *Esther: The NIV Application Commentary.* Grand Rapids, MI: Zondervan Publishing House, 1999.

Kaufman, J., and E. Egan. "Could You Bounce Back?" *Self* (January 2000): p. 129.

Levine, S. *Against Terrible Odds: Lessons in Resilience from Our Children.* Boulder, CO: Bull Publishing Company, 2001.

Martinez, A. "Pioneering CEO Serves as Exemplar for Women." *The Palm Beach Post* (January 28, 2002): p. 1D.

Maxwell, J. C. *Failing Forward: Turning Mistakes into Stepping Stones for Success.* Nashville, TN: Thomas Nelson, 2000.

McCune, J. C., and D. Wallace. "Never Say Die: They Turned Crushing Defeat into Total Victory." *Success* (August 17, 2001): p. 33.

McKanic, P. A. "She's Got the Drive." *Sarasota Herald-Tribune* (July 1, 1998): p. 12.

Michaud, E. "Bouncing Back." *Prevention* (June 2002): p. 110.

Putney, F. M. "Why Me? Physician-Author Jamie Weisman Writes to Seek the Answers." *Atlanta Jewish Times* (July 19, 2002). www.atlantajewishtimes.com/archives/2002/071902cs.htm.

Rubin, B. M. "Secrets of Resilient Women." *Good House-keeping* (January 2000): p. 108.

Sampey, K. "It's How You Respond: Six Persevering Women Receive Enterprise Awards. The Associated Press (July 29, 1998).

Sanders, A. "Moving On—And Up: East Side Entrepreneur Has Overcome Tragedy to Build Schleppers into a Force in Fierce Industry." *The Jewish Week* (June 10, 1998): p. 38.

"SCORE Board Member Linda Novey-White Honored with Avon Women of Enterprise Award." (June 11, 1998).

Seligman, M. *Learned Optimism*. New York: Pocket Books, 1998.

Silverman, E. R. "Is the Glass Half Full?" *Human Resource Executive* (June 2, 2000): p. 78.

Vaughn, S. G. *Half-Empty, Half-Full: Understanding the Psychological Roots of Optimism*. Orlando, FL: Harcourt, 2001.

Weaver, T. "A Case Study of Suffering, Resiliency." *The Milwaukee Journal-Sentinel* (July 21, 2002). www.jsonline.com/enter/books/jul02/60089.asp.

Weisman, J. *As I Live and Breathe: Notes of a Patient Doctor*. New York: North Point Press, 2002.

Winfrey, O. "Be a Queen." In J. Canfield (ed.) *Chicken Soup for the Woman's Soul: 101 Stories to Open the Hearts and Rekindle the Spirits of Women*. Deerfield Beach, FL: Health Communications, Inc., 1996.

Wohlgelernter, E. "No Denying Her Now." *The Jerusalem Post* (June 2, 2000): p. 14.

CHAPTER 9

Let the Story Be Told

"Are Women Responsible for the Glass Ceiling?" *USA Today Magazine* (April 2000). www.findarticles.com/cf_0/m1272/2659_128/61586738/rpint.jhtml.

Benni, C. "The Next Step: How to Land a Promotion." *Meetings and Conventions* (April 2001): p. 49.

Bernstein, A. J., and S. C. Rozen. *Sacred Bull: The Inner Obstacles That Hold You Back and How to Overcome Them.* New York: John Wiley and Sons, 1994.

Corcodilos, N. A. *Ask the Headhunter: Reinventing the Interview to Win the Job.* New York: Plume, 1997.

Droste, T. "Promote Yourself During an Interview." Monster.com. http://adminsupport.monster.com/articles/selling.

Dudley, G. W., and S. Goodson. *The Psychology of Sales Call Reluctance: Earning What You're Worth in Sales.* Dallas, TX: Behavioral Science Research, 1999.

Einhart, N. "Survival Tactic: Recognize Your Female Talent." *Fast Company* (January 2001). www.fastcompany.com/lead/lead_feature/act_fineline.html.

Fox, M. V. *Character and Ideology in the Book of Esther.* Grand Rapids, MI: Wm. B. Eerdman's Publishing Company, 2001.

Gray, C. "Women and Interviews: Career Basics for Women." Ask the Headhunter. www.asktheheadhunter.com/women3.htm.

Jacobs, D. L. "Nice Girls Don't Grandstand." *Working Woman* (March 1995): p. 63.

Kamen, R. "Thinking Out Loud." *The Record* (October 25, 1998): p. E01.

Mallory, M. "Survival Skills." *Atlanta Journal-Constitution* (March 11, 2001): p. R-1.

"New York Post Goodbye Edition Is Locked Away." *Orlando Sentinel Tribune* (September 27, 1990): p. A2.

Pinskey, R. *101 Ways to Promote Yourself: Tricks of the Trade for Taking Charge of Your Own Success.* New York: Avon Books, 1997.

Swiss, D. J. *Women Breaking Through: Overcoming the Final 10 Obstacles at Work.* Princeton, NJ: Petersons Guides, 1997.

CHAPTER 10

Celebrating Your Own Personal Purim

Book, E. W. *Why the Best Man for the Job Is a Woman.* New York: HarperCollins, 2001.

Emerson, B. "Sweet Potato Sisterhood: Books' 'Queenly' Fans Dress Up, Get Down for Some Silly Fun. *The Atlanta Journal-Constitution* (February 17, 2002): p. 1M.

Jobes, K. H. *Esther: The NIV Application Commentary.* Grand Rapids, MI: Zondervan Publishing House, 1999.

Kersey, C. *Unstoppable: 45 Powerful Stories of Perseverance and Triumph from People Just Like You.* Naperville, IL: Sourcebooks, Inc., 1998.

Nash, P. L. "Wild Women: Outrageous Sisterhoods Are Adding Fun and Freedom to the Lives of Local Women." *The News and Record* (December 9, 2001): p. D-1.

Stroup, S. "Queens Show Their True Selves." *The Times-Piscayne* (March 19, 2002): p. 1.

Thomas, M. "The Words That Changed Their Lives." *Bottom Line Personal* (September 1, 2002): p. 9.

Whitney, C. "Fighting for Women." *Ladies' Home Journal* (August 2000). www.findarticles.com/cf_0/m1127/8_117/64564076/print.jhtml.

Winfrey, O. "The Most Fun I Ever Had." *O, The Oprah Magazine* (May 2002).

Yerkes, S. "Out to Sea with Oprah." *San Antonio Express News* (May 19, 1998): p. E-1.

AFTERWORD

An Ancient Archetype for Women Today

Fox, M. V. *Character and Ideology in the Book of Esther.* Grand Rapids, MI: Wm. B. Eerdman's Publishing Company, 2001.

Swindoll, C. R. *Esther: A Woman of Strength and Dignity.* Nashville, TN: Word Publishing, Inc., 1997.

INDEX

Underscored page references indicate boxed text

Accountability, <u>195</u>
Adversity
  handling like a queen, 200
  profiles of courage, 174–84
  resiliency, rules of, 187–88
  spirituality and, 184–86
Ahasuerus, King, 9–11, 13–15
  Esther's plea to, 10–11, 85–88,
      107–10, 129-31, 137, 138, 142, 172
  Haman and, 10–11, 83–84, 147–48
  Queen Vashti and, 9, 14, 70, 141
Alliances, building, 124–28
Audience, playing to, 137, 138

Balance, finding, <u>222</u>
Battles, picking, 142–43
Boards, serving on, 213–14
Body language, 22–24, 27, 33, 133–34
Bosses
  bad, 148–50, <u>158</u>
  control freaks, 150–52
  cutthroats, 152–55
  leaving, 154–55, 167–68
  toxic, 159–60
  tyrants, 155–59
Business card, 213

Catfights, avoiding office, 160–66
Celebration, personal, 220–27
Chip Theory, 164, 166
Command, taking, 114–16
Communication
  Esther's skill in, 129–34, 141
  non-verbal, 22–24, 133–34
  playing to your audience, 137, 138

speech patterns, 132–33
style, matching to interviewer, 32
talking so others will listen, 140–41
Confidence, 28, 29, 39, 206
Confrontation, with
  bosses, 153, <u>158</u>
  coworkers, 163–64
Control freaks, controlling, 150–52
Courage, profiles of, 171–84
Coworkers, dealing with, 160–66, <u>165</u>
Credibility, 31–35, 81–82, 132–33
Credit
  receiving, <u>116</u>
  taking, 210–11, <u>215</u>
Criticism, receiving, <u>135</u>
Culture, understanding corporate,
  16–18
Cutthroats, coping with, 152–55

Detractors, drowning out, 224–25
Dress, for success, 20–22

Entrance, making, 24–25
Esther
  as archetype for women today,
    229–30
  character of, 173–74
  command to Mordecai, 86, 88, 109,
    131–32
  communication skills of, 129–34, 141
  confronting of Haman, 110, 130, 137
  first impression by, 14–15
  gossip use by, 68–69, 79, 80
  mentors of, 37–38, 45, 47–50,
    54–55, 57, 63

Esther *(cont.)*
    modern day lessons of, 5–7
    Mordecai's plea to, 85–88, 114
    plea to King Ahasuerus, 85–88,
        107–10, 129–31, 137, 138, 142, 172
    as role model, 4–5
    secrets, keeping, 81–82, 170
    strategic planning by, 109–10,
        111–12, 114

Failure, fear of, 102–3, 151, 187
Feedback, obtaining, 119

Gossip
    bosses and, 79–81
    confronting spreader of, 78
    engineering positive gossip about
        yourself, 73–93
    Esther's use of, 68–69, 79, 80
    gender differences in, 77, 81
    informative nature of, 71
    motives behind, 77
    negative, 81, 82
    networking for, 72–73
    tapping into office grapevine,
        70–73
    zebra rule, 82

Haman, 10–11, 71, 83–85, 108, 110,
        129–30, 137, 147–48, 171
Hand gestures, excessive, 24
Hegai, 14–15, 16, 37, 45, 47–48, 54–55

Ideas, protecting, 154
Impression, first, 15–16
    body language, 22–24
    confidence, 25
    credibility and, 31–35
    dress, 20–22
    entrance, 24–25
    by Esther, 14–15
    halo effect, 16
    job interview questions and, 19
    presence, executive, 25–31

    reinforcing positive, 30
    understanding corporate culture,
        16–18
Internet, use for
    learning corporate culture, 17
    mentoring, 51
    networking, 125–27
    self-promotion, 213
Interview, job
    credibility, establishing, 32–35
    explaining termination during, 189
    questions, 19
    self-promotion during, 205–6,
        207–10
    thank-you notes, 30
Intuition, trusting, 134–36

Media, use for self-promotion, 214
Mentors, 37–67
    approaching potential, 47, 48
    bosses as, 63
    career-specific, 60
    ending relationships with, 63–65, 66
    Esther and, 37–38, 45, 47–50,
        54–55, 57, 63
    fathers as, 40–43
    female, 52–54
    finding, 45–47
    formal programs, 43–44
    gender differences, 38, 40, 52–56
    from inside the company, 48–49
    male, 54–56
    mentee responsibilities, 65–67
    number of, 58–59, 62
    online, 51
    from outside the company, 49–51
    personality types, contrasting,
        62–63
    radical, 65
    reverse mentoring, 57–58
    seniority of, 56–57
    situational, 60
    symbolic, 61–62
Milestones, marking, 221–23

Mission statement, personal, 111
Mistakes, admitting, <u>195</u>
Morale, employee, 73
Mordecai
    Esther's command to, 86, 88, 109,
        131–32
    Haman and, 10–11, 83, 85
    as mentor, 37–38, 49–50

Negotiations, location of, <u>139</u>
Networking, 124–28. *See also* Gossip
    gender and, 217–18
    for gossip, 72–73
    self-promotion and, 214–18
    with support staff, 76

Optimism, 193–96

Patience, exercising, 29 –31, 111–13
Planning
    alliance building, 124–28
    backup plan, 120–22
    devising a battle plan, 171–20
    by Esther, 109–10, 111–12
    mission statement, personal, 111
    patience, importance of, 111–12
    visibility, increasing, 122–24
    visualizing success, 113
Posture, 22–23, 27
Praising, of colleagues, 77
Presence, executive (royal), 25–31
Promotion. *See* Self-promotion
Protégés, 44, 48, 53, 55, 64, 67. *See also*
    Mentors
Purim, 5, 10–11, 84, 219–20, 225

Quitting a job, 166–67

Resiliency, rules of
    concentrate on goals, 198–99
    failing forward, 188
    leaning on others, 191–93
    lose the victim mentality, 187–88
    make a crisis meaningful, 197–98

    optimism, 193–96
    practice failing, 187
Résumé, 208
Risk
    aversion to, 97–98
    big-picture focus, 103–5
    fear of failure, 102–3
    good and bad, distinguishing,
        100–102
    self-promotion and, 211–12
    taking for success, 98–100
    to whistleblowers, 97–98
Role models, 52, 61. *See also* Mentors
Rules, working around, 117

Secretaries, influence exerted by, 76–77
Secrets, keeping, 81–82
Self-promotion, <u>209</u>
    during job interview, 205–10
    methods, 210–18
    powerplays, 210
    problems with, 202–4
    in résumé, 208
    women's trouble with, 204–5
Sneak attack, use of, 114
Speaking up, importance of, 114–15,
    140–41, 212
Speech patterns, 132–33
Spirituality, role in recovery from
    adversity, 185
Supporters, thanking, 223–24
Support staff, building relationships
    with, 76–77

Thank-you notes, <u>30,</u> 76
Timing, value of, 134
Tyrants, bosses as, 155–59

Vashti, Queen, 9, 14, 70, 141
Victim mentality, 187–88
Visibility, 122–24, 207, <u>209</u>, 213
Visualizing success, 113

Whistleblowers, 88–97, <u>96</u>

ABOUT THE AUTHORS

CONNIE GLASER is one of the country's top authorities on women in the workplace. A sought-after guest on TV and radio, she has appeared on *The Today Show*, CNN, *Bloomberg News*, and *NBC Nightly News*.

A nationally recognized speaker and consultant, her client list includes AT&T, AOL Time Warner, Hewlett-Packard, Johnson & Johnson, PricewaterhouseCoopers, Office Depot, and the U.S. Navy. She also serves as National Spokesperson for the Business Women's Network, representing the interests of over 30 million women world-wide.

Connie was recently honored by being named Businesswoman of the Year by Office Depot. She has also been named to the *World Who's Who of Women*. She lives in Atlanta with her husband and two sons, where she is a featured columnist for the *Atlanta Business Chronicle*.

BARBARA STEINBERG SMALLEY has been a successful freelance writer for nearly twenty years. Her specialty is writing for and about women, and she has published more than five hundred articles in national magazines such as *Woman's Day*, *Redbook*, *Woman's World*, and *Reader's Digest*.

Recently, Barbara was a recipient of the prestigious ATHENA Award, an international award that recognizes women who selflessly give of their time and talents to help other women reach their goals. She lives in Athens, Georgia, with her husband and two children.

What Queen Esther Knew
Keynote Speeches • Seminars • Workshops

Connie Glaser is a dynamic and inspiring speaker. She is available for keynote presentations and seminars based on *What Queen Esther Knew* or other issues related to women in business. For more information, visit her Web site at **www.connieglaser.com.**

Here's what some of Connie's clients have to say:

"Thank you! Thank you! What else can I say? Your presentation was an astounding success and your dynamic style captivated the group. I know that other organizations would certainly benefit from your timely message and motivating presence."
—**Barbara Binkley,** Deloitte & Touche

"Thank you for an outstanding presentation filled with humor, insight, and relevance. My only regret is that the time went by so quickly. We could have listened for at least another hour!"
—**Lucille Luongo,** American Women in Radio & Television

"Your praises have been sung far and wide by past participants. And when I notified our employees that we were going to offer your course again, I had so many requests that I had to place people on waiting lists!"
—**Kathleen Charles,** Human Resources, State of Georgia